Preface

With the change in fishing regulations on many of this provinces trout waters heading toward a no-bait restriction, I felt it was important to write a book explaining some different techniques for alternative methods of catching fish. I have included a brief introduction for beginners on equipment requirements and "how to fish" methods that will help them get started in the sport.

There are different types of habitat and environments that trout and other fish live in, so I have covered some of this in the first chapters of the book. It can be a daunting task trying to figure out what type of angling methods to use on different trout waters, so hopefully this information will help you make your choice.

Through my life time of fishing the area waters mentioned in this book, I have developed a special interest in contributing back into the resource that I have taken so much from, in particular the area fishery and the habitat in which my beloved trout live. As a result, I have tried to make time to get involved in some very interesting projects to benefit the fishery. I have mentioned a few of these in some of the chapters as well.

There have been some major changes in the way that anglers think about fishing these days. Conservation has become an important part of our thoughts and conversation when it comes to angling. This is good! It is up to use to help look after the resource and in doing so the benefits can be very rewarding.

We have started to slowly evolve from a "live off the land" mentality that was so typical for our ancestors. Recreational sport angling is as it implies, a "form of recreation", not a way of feeding the family. However, there are plenty of stocked lakes out there that are managed for a harvest and you can still take a few home for the frying pan.

Fishing These Parts

By - Guy Woods

Illustrations and cover photos by Guy Woods
Book photos – Glenbow museum, Guy Woods
Prints – Alberta Environment, TransAlta Utilites Corp., Sports Scene Publications Inc.

Published by - Bow Valley Habitat Development

BVHD Environmental Ltd.
#5 Glenport Road
Cochrane, Alberta T4C 1G8

e-mail guywoods@telusplanet.net

Printed in China

Table of Contents

Acknowledgements

I would like to acknowledge and thank all of the GOOD Provincial, Federal, NGO and Corporate fisheries biologists that I have had the good fortune to work with over the years! I am forever grateful for their commitment and support to the fisheries resource. I have benefited from their willingness to share their knowledge and I have been inspired by their enthusiasm. In particular, the late Bill Griffiths, with whom I fished, hunted and worked with for a much too brief period time.

Dedication

This book is dedicated to the next generation of outdoor enthusiasts that will learn to love and enjoy the fisheries resource and the environment in which they live. It is my hope that their enjoyment of the resource will help shape them into the future stewards of the environment that we all appreciate.

Above Photo: Young angler Kirsty Yates with her first fish.

Introduction

There are three primary attractions that keep me interested in sport fishing. Number one is; I just love to fish. Number two is the desire to acquire more knowledge about the sport and the third is the desire to explore new fishing water. Along the way, an angler can pick up little tidbits of information about some new potential fishing spots or an almost secret method of catching incredible numbers of fish. Over time, long lasting memories are collected, thoughts of past outings and the environment in which the sport was enjoyed. These are just a few of my own personal interests in sport fishing, there are many more that add to the overall experience.

I have been a fly fisherman for over thirty years now, but I have not forgotten my roots. My first experience fishing the banks of the Bow River in Cochrane, Alberta, involved an inexpensive Zebco rod and reel, a can of worms, and a lot of patience. However, times have changed, new fishing regulations restricting the use of bait to capture sport fish are in place on many waters. The new guidelines were designed to protect our wild sport fish fishery in a modern era and insure the survival of the resource for future generations.

The sport fishing opportunities in the Province of Alberta in the present day are managed to provide the best possible angling experience for all of those that enjoy it, yet at the same time protect and maintain the fishery for the future. Many lakes are stocked annually with sport fish from

1

provincially operated fish hatcheries, to ensure recreation for Alberta anglers. Many of these lakes are defined as put and take fisheries, and the regulation guidelines on them allow limited harvest of sport fish.

The most common sport fish planted in a put and take lake fishery is the rainbow trout. Because rainbow trout do not reproduce in a lake environment, the trout are stocked with the intention of allowing an annual harvest by anglers. The trout that are caught are not wild trout, so the use of bait is allowed in the harvest methods.

Other exemptions to the bait fishing regulation are made for sport fish to encourage harvest of certain species. Such is the case with the Rocky Mountain whitefish. Presently, during the late summer and fall of the year, anglers are allowed the use of maggots for bait while angling for mountain whitefish.

For most flowing waters in the Province, where wild trout reside, the use of bait is not permitted. Along with the new Province wide ban on barbed hooks, the bait ban on most waters allows the safe release of caught sport fish. In order to learn the regulations that guide anglers thru the do's and don'ts of fishing in the Province, you are advised to read the guide to sport fishing regulations that are published annually by the Province. Under today's present fishing regulation you are required to possess an Alberta sport fishing license if you are 16 to 64 years of age. For those that do not require a fishing license, you are still responsible to comply with the rules of the game, so make sure you read the regulations, they are free of charge.

These new age restrictions on the methods in which we can use to catch fish, have led to a demand for more information directed toward alternative fishing techniques that will help fill the gap left by "bait bans" and produce positive results on streams and lakes. Presently, the only alternative angling method most commonly considered when faced with a no bait regulation, is the use of lures such as jigs, spoons, spinners and artificial flies. Without the effective use of a fly rod for casting artificial flies, it is commonly accepted that jigs, spoons or spinners are the only option in lures for fishing, using a spinning or spin casting rod. However, based on my own personal past experience this is not necessarily the case!

I learned earlier on in my angling experience that drifting a baited stonefly along the bottom of the riverbed using a spin casting rod and reel, light line and the right size split shot weight, was a deadly method for catching trout and mountain whitefish. Today, as a fly fisherman, I still use the same method on the river, except that instead of a baited stonefly and spin casting rod, I'm casting an artificial stonefly and using a fly rod to deliver my offering.

It has been a common practice on many British Columbia lakes for years, to troll a streamer behind a boat using a spinning rod and a split shot for weight, to catch large rainbow trout. Most fly fishers practice the same technique casting or trolling a sinking fly line from a boat or float tube. The methods used to present the artificial fly are different, but the results are often the same.

The use of artificial fishing flies is too often considered an angling method designed specifically for the fly rod caster and not for the spin casting enthusiast or beginner. For young toddlers, their first fishing experience may turn to disaster if you try and start them off with a spinner or spoon. The use of a bobber and fly is a good way to get children started without over complicating their experience on the first outing.

In this book I will cover some of the basic information that you will need to know to get started in sport fishing. The following chapters will cover the best basic equipment that you will need along with how to fish different types of water and some of the best methods for doing so. I will also cover a variety of ice fishing techniques that I have used with success over the years.

It is hoped that the angling methods mentioned in this book for using an artificial fly on a spinning or spin casting rod will result in a new adventure in your fishing experience. Ultimately, you may end up with a fly rod in your hands.

Above Photo: A young boy travels the banks of the Bow River while fishing in the Town of Cochrane, Alberta.

Part One

Fishing Equipment

Depending on your age and ability with equipment, different types of fishing rods and reels are required in sport angling. Today, there are very reasonably priced rod and reel combos available to the beginning angler. Compared to other sports, basic fishing is a very inexpensive sport to enter into.

Toddlers

For young children, the secret is to keep their fishing equipment simple. Rods, reels, line and tackle should be basic and easy to use. I recommend a short light fishing rod designed to hold a smaller sized spin casting reel. Spin casting reels are by far the easiest piece of angling equipment that a child can get their hands on. The reel has a cover over the line spool to prevent tangles and a button devise on the back of the reel for easy casting.

Line quality and size are very important in the overall package. I have witnessed young anglers trying to cast a light tackle set up using heavy test line, the result was major frustration and line tangles. The word test is used to describe the strength of the line, and represents the weight in which the line will break under a stress "test". Spools of line are sold in 4.lb, 6.lb, 8.lb etc. or in the same strength in metric measurements. Heavier line, especially the cheaper versions, has a tendency to come off of the reel in coil's, this coiling is called line memory. Line memory interferes with the line passing thru the line guides on the rod and has a negative impact on casting.

My recommendation for a good overall line weight for most trout and mountain whitefish fishing would be 6.lb test. A good quality line will mention on the packaging that it has low memory. This lighter line will allow easy casting, it is thin enough to fool most fish that are suspicious and line shy, and it's plenty strong enough to land some pretty large fish. All fishing reels are equipped with drag systems built into their design, if your drag adjustment is set properly, the stress point of the lighter line can be avoided. By playing or tiring a fish using your fishing rod and your drag combined, it is surprising how durable modern day light weight fishing lines are made.

Once you have made your choice of line, rod and reel for the beginning toddler, you must consider the proper care the equipment to insure that it makes it to the water and home again in one piece. This is often overlooked by many parents, and can result in a broken rod tip or damaged reel. Rod and reel cases are a good investment in the long run. There are cases in the market place that include a reel cover built into the design, so that you can pack your rod and reel into the case assembled.

A cheaper alternative that I have used in past year's, is to purchase a length of PVC plastic pipe with two end caps. Most fishing rods come in two piece attachable sections, which will reduce the length of plastic pipe that you require. However, you must remove the reel in order to properly store the fishing rod. When you do separate the reel from the rod on a spin casting setup, make sure to leave a length of line out of the reel, you can use a piece of tape or an elastic band to attach the tag end of the line to the reel. If the reel is wet after your outing, make sure you let the reel dry out before you stow it away.

Adults and teenagers

For those more advanced in the sport or entering it at a more mature age, spinning rod and reel combos are the best choice of equipment. Many spinning rods and reels that are sold today are designed for specific angling applications, such as casting heavy lures and catching large fish. In Canada, pike fishing combos are very common in fishing equipment stores. While shopping for your equipment, consider the type of fishing that you are most likely to enjoy.

If it is trout and mountain whitefish that you are after, you will definitely be better off with a light rod and reel combo. Remember, most angling applications will only require 6.lb test line and about 100 m on your spool. There is no point in spooling a reel with 100m of 6.lb test, if the reel was designed for 100m of 20.lb test. Spinning reels usually mention on their packaging or on the spool, the length of a particular test line that can be added to the spool on the reel.

When you graduate into spinning equipment, the choice of rod that you want to use is the most important one. Different rod lengths are best suited to different types of water and what angling method that you are using. Spinning rods and fishing rods in general, come in different lengths, weights and actions. The action of a fishing rod refers to its relative stiffness, and is defined as fast action (stiff tip section), medium fast (semi-stiff tip section), and medium action (medium stiff tip section), with some of the slower flexing rods defined as slow and parabolic action. My choice for fishing a river would be a long light rod with a medium fast action. For small streams and narrow willow covered creeks, I like a short light weight rod.

How long is long and how short is short you ask? You will be hard pressed to find a light weight spinning rod over 7 feet, except for noodle rods, which should not be ruled out as a good choice. The short light weight rods are more common, and come in 5.5 foot, 6.0 foot etc. After reading some of the angling methods that I reveal in this book, you may have a better understanding of why a long rod is important on big water.

When I acquired my first fly rod, much of its use was enjoyed with a spinning reel in the rod seat at the base of the rod. The fly rod was 8 foot 6 inches long, and it worked perfectly on the banks of the Bow River for drifting a fly or a baited hook. The rod tip was sensitive enough to detect the slightest bump on the bottom of the river or in the jaws of a hunger trout or whitefish.

I graduated up to a spinning reel after my old Zebco reel fell apart on a gravel road while walking back from the Bow River. I was sorry to find out that the reel, after many years of use, was beyond repair. However, I was content in knowing the many years of use that I had enjoyed with such an inexpensive rod and reel combo. By that time in my angling life I was ready to move up to equipment that would meet the demands of the user.

I will not go into the use of bait casting rods and reels for fishing in this book. The bait casting system is designed primarily for casting heavier lures, and it can be used effectively for fishing for larger fish than the trout and whitefish. Members of the trout family and whitefish are the focus in the fishing techniques mentioned in this book. If you are already familiar with this system of casting, it can be used in some applications using weighted streamers for large trout, walleye and pike.

Much of our angling season is restricted to ice fishing on area lakes and reservoirs, with this in mind, it is important to cover the type of equipment designed specifically for this fishing method. Today, there is a wide variety of equipment available for fishing thru the ice. Rods built for this purpose are very short in length and will accommodate the same reels that you use during the fair weather season. Fishing with reels in sub-zero weather is hard on the mechanics of your equipment, icing on the reel can lead to problems with normal operation and lubricants used on the internal gears can stiffen.

Fishing lines that are manufactured for fair weather fishing can be problematic when used thru the ice. I prefer too use a slightly heavier test during the winter months to compensate. Instead of the normal 6.lb test, I switch to 8.lb. However, there are special lines available for ice fishing in the market place today. These ice fishing lines are more abrasion resistant and have less line memory under sub-zero conditions.

If you can afford the expense, you can purchase separate equipment specifically designed for winter ice fishing. I have noticed that there is a wide range of inexpensive rod – reel combo's available in some of the leading sporting goods stores and major chain store departments. The reels on these outfits are relatively small compared to normal season reels, but they do the job intended on most trout and whitefish that you will angle for.

Basic Tackle

When you have acquired a good rod, reel and line for the angling that you wish to do, you will have to equip yourself with some basic tackle to complete your outfitting. Basic tackle covers a wide spectrum of choices that require different tackle storage systems for your stuff. If you are going to be fishing from a boat, a tackle box or bag may be adequate for your storage needs. On rivers and streams, where you will probably be using smaller lures, leaders and weights, a good method of traveling equipped could involve the purchase of a tackle fishing vest.

Tackle boxes or bags are great if you are fishing from a fixed position, but if you plan on walking the banks of a stream, the less equipment that you have to carry, the more time you'll have to concentrate on fishing. Fishing vests are relatively inexpensive and light weight. A vest will allow you quick and east access to everything you need. A small pair of nail clippers and pliers can be attached to the outside of the vest for tackle changes.

There will be some basic fishing tackle options mentioned in this book, but by far the best tips that you can receive over time are those that you will pick up at the local sporting goods store, or by talking to fellow anglers on the water. The best formula for success in this sport is communication. If I had not been open to suggestions from sporting goods employees, or interested in talking to fellow anglers over the years, it could have been a long lonely road to becoming a competent angler.

When the opportunity to talk to other anglers on streams, rivers or lakes has presented itself, I am a willing and eager participate. These encounters have been to my benefit, increasing my knowledge of fishing. If I ever walked away without learning any new tips about how and where to catch fish, at least I have gained in sharing my enthusiasm for fishing with a fellow angler. When you are having a great day, it is a please to share the experience.

Fishing nets are often overlooked when fishing equipment is the focus of a beginning angler, yet it is probably one of the more important tools of the sport. A good fishing net can assist the angler in the safe capture and release of wild trout or insure the landing of a stocked trout or whitefish when the frying pan is waiting. There are modern nets that are designed to lessen the impact of the capture of sport fish for safe release. These release nets are made of a soft synthetic mesh for general use or rubber for boat anglers.

If you are a boat angler, you will be in the market for a net with a long handle for dipping from a distance. Stream and river nets are short in design and often equipped with an elastic rope that can be attached to a vest. One of the nets that I have is a folding net that can be coiled into a small diameter and stored in a belt case. I like this particular net for fishing small streams and creeks where the willows are thick and snagging a loose net can be frustrating. A net is a good investment and can be a helpful tool for many years into the future; this should be considered when you purchase your first net.

Fishing waders for crossing streams and wading closer to potential fish habitat are an important part of the sport. The purchase of waders by a beginner is often left until later on, when an angler becomes familiar with the types of water they are going to spend the most angling time on. If your destination is big water, like the Bow River, waders are a major advantage. However, there are important safety concerns involved in wading big water rivers like the Bow River. The safe and effective use of waders on flowing and still waters is a primary consideration in the sport.

Once you are comfortable with the environment in which you plan on spending most of your time fishing, you should consult with a knowledge-able sporting goods employee to determine the best and safest choice of wader to use while on the water. One should never under estimate the power of flowing water, and it will take time to learn to read water and understand flow velocities from the shoreline, before you enter the water. The use of a personal floatation devise should be considered for any big water wading.

I have talked to a number of anglers that have had close calls while wading big water over the years. Some of them explained that they were lucky to still be around after they survived their accident.

Above Photo: Angler Eric Schumann hooks into a nice brown trout on the Dogpound Creek.

Part Two

Fishing a Fly on a Casting Rod

The stretch of Bow River that flows thru my home town of Cochrane is influenced by variable flow volumes from the Ghost Reservoir power facility approximately 20 km upstream. When there is a daytime demand for hydro power electricity, the Ghost dam releases large volumes of water to operate the generators in the power plant. During non-demand hours of the day, the plant releases a smaller volume of water into the river that results in low flow conditions. The water levels in the river in Cochrane usually start to rise around 11.00 AM in the morning.

When I was a young boy fishing the Bow River's deeper pools and runs early in the day, during these low flow periods, I would always make sure to keep an eye open for any snagged lures. The lures would be found tangled in the streambed rocks and had been lost during high water flows on previous days by some unfortunate angler. However, their loss turned out to be my gain, and I found that I was soon accumulating a substantial collection of hooks and lures.

This collection of a wide variety of spinners, spoons, hooks and weights led to my first experience with spin fishing. I remember my preferred choice of lures was small bladed spinners and small spoons that were effective lures for the resident rainbows, cutthroat and occasional brown trout. All fly hooks that were found had to be almost free of rust before they made it into my respectable collection. The trout flies that I found back in those days consisted pretty much exclusively of wet flies. Among my find were such old classic favorites such as royal coachman's, lead wing coachman's, black knat, cow dung, march brown, silver professors and so on.

Although these famous classic trout flies were designed for trout, I always did better with them while fishing for whitefish using a worm or maggot for bait. Especially during the fall run of rocky mountain whitefish in the Bow River. Every fall in early September, the mountain whitefish would move up the river and stage into shallower runs, getting ready to spawn. If there weren't any stone flies to bait on a bare hook, I wound set up my line with a wet fly at the end and a small nail or split shot for weight. The weight was place about 2 feet up from the fly.

One of my favorite techniques for catching whitefish was to stand at the top of an eddy in the current, and cast the wet fly out and across the current. When the fly swung around into the eddy line, I would hold it in position and wait for a bite. I feel a little guilty when I think back on how many whitefish ended up on my stringer or forked willow. Back in those days, conservation was not a major issue in my mind, and the legal daily catch limits were more than substantial.

One of the limiting factors to beginner fly fishers in the town of Cochrane in those day's, was the lack of a good selection of more effective trout flies that could be fished without the use of bait. When I started to learn from some of the more experience fly fisherman that frequented the Bow River, they showed me a selection of good patterns to try. This newly gained knowledge was a major contributing influence in my use of effective trout flies as a choice fishing lure. My collection of trout flies began to grow.

However, it wasn't until I started using a fly rod more often and started tying my own flies that learned some of the secrets in catching trout and whitefish consistently. Much of my fly fishing time these days is dedicated to the use of the wet fly. There are three types of wet flies used in this type of fishing, nymphs, streamers and traditional wet fly's. From what I have learned thru experience, the methods used in fishing these three different types of wet flies with a fly rod, can also be applied to fishing with spin casting or spinning rods and reels.

The availability of good quality wet flies today has opened new doors to beginner anglers. The cost of using artificial flies is less expensive than spoons or spinners and the variety of flies to select from is incredible. When one considers the fly fishing option to catch fish there is a common understanding that an angler needs to spend a substantial amount of money to get started as a fly fisher. This is the dilemma if you consider the standard equipment required to become a fully outfitted fly fisher, but if you're a spin fisher that wishes to fish wet flies on monofilament line, this is not the case.

A large part of the fly fishing experience involves dry fly fishing. Dry fly fishing lines are designed to present the fly using the weight of the line for casting and it works very effectively doing just that. The techniques involved in fishing a wet fly with monofilament line can not be used effectively for casting the dry fly. I have never spent much time exploring this approach, but I can recall witnessing an interesting attempt that seemed quite effective for the angler that was using a dry fly setup with a spinning rod and reel.

In the early 1960's my fishing buddies and I would spend countless hours fishing the Bighill creek just north of town. This small creek was full of stocked rainbow trout, brown trout and eastern brook trout in different areas along its course. Our favorite spots to fish were the numerous beaver dams that were located within easy walking or biking distance from our homes.

From year to year the creek was always a good fishing spot to spend a summer's day trying to catch a limit. We would use bait, spinners, spoons and wet flies trying to hook a good size rainbow trout or what ever, including suckers.

One evening, a car pulled up on the road that bordered the creek and parked next to a large beaver dam that was always one of our favorite spots. My friend and I were fishing the far side of the beaver dam across from the man that climbed the fence and found a spot next to the water. The man waved a greeting; we waved back and then watched as he sat down next to his rod and tackle box. In those days it was impolite to talk or yell and scare the fish, so we new that he was an experienced fisherman.

After watching him sitting there, watching the water for some time, I began to wonder if he had forgot his bait or something. The air was dead calm and silent enough to hear the swarming mosquitoes and midges hovering over the water. You could also hear the disturbance of rising trout up the length of the beaver dam. Soon after a few trout had risen close to his position, the man started rummaging thru his tackle box and then setting up his spinning rod and line.

I lost track of his activities until I heard the sound of his bobber hit the water some minutes after. The fisherman had rigged up his line with a bobber and three flies in a method that I had never witness before. On the end of his monofilament line was a clear narrow bobber that was stream-lined in shape. Up from the float about three feet was a selection of three fly hooks attached to the main line with short leaders of varying lengths and spaced about 1 foot apart. The fly that was closest to the bobber was shorter than the two farthest away.

From a distance it appeared that the flies were all dry flies. After the fisherman made a long cast upstream, onto the slick surface of the dam, he would hold his rod tip high in the air and slowly reel in while wiggling his rod tip. By keeping his rod tip at the right height during this method of fishing, all three flies would dance on the surface of the water, up from the float. By the time the man had decided to leave the creek, later in the evening, our favorite beaver dam fishing hole was missing about 4 of its better sized rainbows. The fisherman had also caught and released a number of smaller trout in the process.

This technique of dancing dry flies on the surface of the water is used by fly fishers when fishing close to the top of the bank of deep runs, on creeks with plenty of shore cover. It is called dapping. The fly fisher uses a short leader on the fly line and wiggles the end of their fly rod, to create this dancing presentation. I learned about this ancient technique of fishing, many years later. Back at the time, I was impressed with technique so much that if I had owned any dry flies, I would have been trying the method after the angler on the beaver dam that evening had landed his second trout.

It is common knowledge among experienced fly fishers that a trout's diet consists of around 90 % nymphs and larva. This would indicate that much of a trout's feeding time is spent feeding on nymphs and larva. Some of the larger trout will prefer targeting small fish and large aquatic invertebrates like leeches. For this reason, wet flies are the anglers best bet for success on most outings. Even when trout turn to dry flies to feed, many of them are taking emerging nymphs, just below the surface, at the same time.

Fly fishers do their best to imitate this food supply by fishing fly patterns that are tied to represent the aquatic life that the fish are feeding on. The flies are created from feathers, fur, yarn and other synthetic materials that are tied onto hooks designed for this purpose. The presentation of the fly is very important in the fishing of the fly.

Presentation of an artificial fly translates into the proper placement of the fly in the water, the correct movement and depth at which the fly is fished. Sometimes no movement of the fly is required. In most applications when fishing flowing water, a dead drift of the fly is the preferred presentation. However, like small fish or leeches, some nymphs are swimmers and a controlled movement of the artificial fly is used to imitate them.

Still water fishing in lakes, ponds or reservoirs provides an angler with a totally different angling experience. Aquatic insects in lakes are different in nature compared to those in flowing water. In still water any movement an insect makes can attract the eye of a predator, so much of the aquatic life moves very slowly. Presenting a fly suspended from a strike indicator or a bobber, at the right depth and without any movement is sometimes the most effective way to fish.

Where fly fishers use different types of floating and sinking line to present a fly, a spin caster or spinning fisher must improvise his or her angling techniques to gain the same results. This can be achieved by using bobbers and split shot weights. When I say bobbers I'm not talking about your average store bought variety of fixed position bobber. Slip bobbers are the only float devise that will work effectively in both flowing and still water fly fishing techniques when you are using monofilament line.

Slip Bobbers

Slip bobbers have been around for a very long time, and they are readily available in most sporting goods and major retail department stores. The float is long and narrow in design, with a small diameter hole thru a tube in its center. The slender design of the slip bobber allows the angler to retrieve the float along the surface of the water without creating very much of a disturbance in the surface tension. The mono-line is thread thru the hole and allows the bobber to slide up and down the length of the line, thus the word slip bobber. In order to stop the bobber at a given point along the line, a bobber stop is used.

The bobber is first threaded onto the line, and then a fly and weight is tied on the end of the line. By placing a bobber stop at different points on the main line, an angler can control the depth at which the weight and fly is fished. If the bobber stop is the correct one, it will easily pass thru the rod guides easily when the line is cast or when it is reeled in, at the same time the slip bobber will slide down the line to the weight, ready for the next cast.

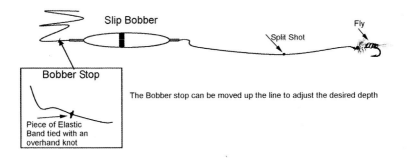

The Bobber stop can be moved up the line to adjust the desired depth

A good bobber stop to use in this fishing method is a small elastic band tied onto the monofilament line with a simple overhand knot and then trimmed with clippers. This setup allows an angler to easily cast the fly, weight and bobber, from a short fishing rod. As soon as the fly hits the water, the fly and weight sink while the bobber slides up the line to the stop, which holds the fly and weight at the proper depth.

The elastic stop can be easily adjusted to different points on the line to attain different depths for the fly. This technique can be used in both flowing and still water applications. In deep water fishing, using this method of suspending the fly, you can get down to depths of 20 or more feet with ease.

Line Stripping

When movement is necessary in the presentation of a wet fly in lakes and streams there is another method that works good using monofilament line and a casting reel. Placing a split shot of the right weight about 3 feet up from a chosen wet fly without a bobber, will allow the angler to cast the fly to the desired distance for a moving retrieve, at a given depth and with the right action.

Fly fishers use a variety of line stripping methods or slow steady retrieves to add life like motion to the fly. This same method of giving action to the fly can be achieved using a casting rod and reel. By manipulating the rod tip as you reel in you can create a short jerking motion of the fly or a long slow stripping retrieve. If it's a slow steady movement that is required, a slow reeling action is the answer. This is where the choice of rod length and stiffness can play an important role in your line retrieve options. A longer rod with a faster action will make the task easier to achieve.

Split Shot

Streamer Fly

High Sticking

In flowing streams and rivers, the use of a float is the easiest method for dead drifting a wet fly. There is another more complex technique for presenting a fly on a dead drift that I first used when I got my first fly rod. It is even more effective for keeping the fly at the right depth during a drift but requires a bit more attention. Its most useful application is when you are nymph fishing flowing water right in front of you. To use this method properly, you need a long light weight rod and a good selection of various sizes of split shot weights.

In fly fishing circles it is referred to as "high sticking"-- an appropriate Canadian label for sure! The technique involves casting your nymph and weight upstream, and by keeping your rod tip high with a length of free line in your other hand, you can control the depth of the fly as it drifts downstream in front of you. Ideally, if your weight is the correct size for a given current in the water, the fly and weight will bounce along the bottom without snagging in the rocks. Any hits or bites from fish are usually noticeable and become more so with experience.

To use this same method with a monofilament casting rod and reel, you should use a long rod. Once you have the required length of line off of the reel, you should not have to use the reel to cast. The line in your free hand and out the end of the long rod will be adequate for flipping the fly back upstream after every drift. This method is called flipping. The technique requires a little more skill than bobber fishing, but when you master it your catch rates will improve substantially.

When I first started using this system of catching fish, I found that a spinning reel that was the best choice, especially for the casting options. In fast flowing rivers like the middle and upper Bow River, trout and whitefish often hold in eddies or runs close to shore, and a long cast was not necessary. Using the free line in my left hand to flip the fly upstream made the method a very fast way of covering a lot of water without much effort. Once the fly and weight were downstream at the end of the drift, the current is used to load the rod and flip the fly and split shot back upstream.

This flip casting the fly is a great way to fish small creeks with plenty of shore cover. By holding a given length of line by your free hand you have more control in your casting, and in most cases on small creeks the required cast, in tight cover, is usually a short one. If you are fishing from an upstream position, you can feed more line off of the reel as the fly drifts downstream in the current. Then on the retrieve, the line can be recovered by reeling in the excess.

Fishing a Streamer with a Spoon

In 2007, I was under contract to do some work for Alberta Sustainable Resources and I was staying at a Forestry Camp in the Livingstone Creek area. There were crews of Forestry people staying in the camp, some to complete Forestry work programs and a fire crew was underway on a training program.

With the camp located just across the road from the Oldman River, I had brought my fly rod to pass the evenings fishing for cutthroat and rainbow trout that resided in the Oldman and a few other area streams. It was mid July and there were plenty of hatches happening on all of the streams in the area.

As soon as I arrived at the camp, I met a young man that was interested in learning how to cast a fly rod. He had brought one with him but he hadn't had any lessons to get off on the right foot. I agreed to show him some basic casting techniques and possibly fish with him once he got a start. After a few minutes of instruction around the helicopter field, I left him to practice his casting and started walking back across the road to the main camp.

There was a camp of fire fighters right next to the heliport that had been watching us cast and I met four young lads heading out to fish just as I got to the road. They were equipped with pop cans wrapped with monofilament line and a small fishing spoon for a lure on the end of each line. They were going to use these basic fishing tools to catch some trout on the river, just down the road. We parted ways after a little conversation and I headed back to my truck to head out fishing myself.

After loading my fishing gear in the truck I drove about 1 km down the road to a small trail that started at the edge of the ditch. Driving down the trail I came within metres of a high bank and path that led down to the river. I had just put on my fly fishing vest, when up from the path down the steep bank came two of the young men that I had met just 30 minutes earlier.

We talk for a few minutes about some of the fly fishing gear that I was using; they seemed very interested in this method fishing. When I stated that it was time to travel upstream to fish, one of the fellows ask me if I would mind if they joined me to watch me cast a fly. I said "not a problem"; I would enjoy the company if they stayed downstream of me while I fished.

Soon after I started fishing, the other two friends that had been fishing with their pop cans downstream, joined us. I came to a very good looking run on a side channel of the Oldman River, just upstream from where I started to fish. It was a long deep channel that started below a riffle and a rock out cropping 30 m upstream. It was a perfect piece of dry fly water that I was determined to catch a trout out of.

As I moved up the run, the four anglers below me followed through with their spoons, casting across the channel and wrapping the line back onto the pop cans as they did their retrieve. I had learned of this fishing technique years earlier, when I had traveled to Mexico.

The Mexican kids would cast their heavy monofilament line off of pop cans while fishing the ocean shoreline. They would hold the pop can with line in their one hand, while they whorled the bait and sinker to cast with their other hand. The line would slip off of the pop can just like the spool on a spin casting reel.

One of the anglers that had joined me had prefect control of his line, using this fishing method. His casts were very accurate, just off of the bank on the opposite side of the channel on every cast. When he wrapped the line back onto the pop can on his retrieve, he did so with a short jerking or jigging motion.

I was casting a dry stonefly imitation on my fly rod and as I neared the riffle at the head of the run, a large rainbow trout took the pattern. The rainbow made some high jumps, clearing the water in rapid succession. The four fellow anglers ran up to my side to witness the battle. As I brought the trout to the net, I was asked by one of the young men if I was going to eat it. I said no, I'm going to release the fish.

After asking me a number of times if he could have the trout to eat, I told him that he would have to catch his own fish. I reassured him that trout always taste better if they are caught by the cook and "diner". He was very disappointed when I let the large trout slip back into the water.

Soon after that first trout, I caught a nice sized cutthroat trout in the same piece of water. I also released the fish. By this time, all four of my

16

companions were dead serious about catching their own trout to eat. One of them asked me if they could buy the same fly pattern that I was using from my selection, to put on the end of their monofilament line. I explained that they would not be able to cast out the fly without a bobber for a casting weight.

However, I did offer to give one of them a streamer pattern to try. I advised them that a streamer could be used with the weight of the spoon that they were using as a casting weight and as an attractor to bring trout in for a look. I had used this method of fishing a streamer when I was younger and found it to be a very effective method of catching trout.

I told the young angler to take his treble hook off of the spoon and I would give him a short length of 6.lb monofilament leader and a streamer pattern to tie onto the end of the spoon. The trailing streamer would follow the action of the spoon on the retrieve, just like some anglers use "Willow Leafs", "Flashers" or "Ford Fenders" for; while trolling in lakes for trout or in the ocean for salmon.

It wasn't five minutes after the angler started fishing with this method, that he caught a nice trout. When they left the river that evening, they had caught 2 nice trout for the frying pan. They had also learned a new method of catching trout that would be put to use in the coming days over the summer's evenings.

The four young men were very appreciative of what I had taught them. We developed a friendship over the following days. Three of them were from the Blackfoot nation and one was a Stoney from just west of Cochrane. I knew some of the Stoney angler's relatives. After I had finished my contract, on the evening before I was to leave camp, the four young men with one of their elders came up to my cabin. The elder thanked me for helping the young men catch trout. I explained that it had been my pleasure to both fish with them and that I had enjoyed their company.

This method of fishing a streamer fly pattern behind a spoon or spinner is a simple yet effective method of catching trout in both streams and lakes. The leader should be kept relatively short in length, about two feet on stream applications and about 3 feet on lakes. The choice of spoon color or size is up to you. I find that small 1'" too 2" spoons and spinners are about right. You don't want to scare the trout away with too big an attractor.

On both spoons and spinners, it is important to have a swivel on the upper end of the lure to prevent line from twisting. Also, there is a circle clip that attaches the treble hook to the lure. Leave this on to allow a good knot when you attach the leader. If you attempt to tie the leader onto the hole in the spoon, you will create a weak spot in your set up.

The action created by the spoon will help add a seductive movement in your fly pattern. I have never tried this method of angling with a flat fish lure but I'm confident that it would produce good results. The same holds true for small minnow imitating plugs that deep dive when trolled submerged and retrieved on a cast.

Fishing Tight Cover

Small trout baring creeks are often bordered by thick willow cover that makes the fly fishing option a challenge. I have fished many creeks that fit the bill, and I have encountered great difficulty in trying to manipulate a fly rod to present my fly properly. Outside of fishing the odd beaver dam or open area that may hold trout, much of the trout holding water is almost inaccessible for the fly fisher. When you do find a likely spot with an approach to present a fly, you must exercise all of your accumulated knowledge and patience in getting your fly to where the trout are.

I can think of one such experience that comes to my mind when I think of tough closed cover fishing on a small creek. The location of my outing was the upper reaches of Dogpound Creek back in the 1980's. The particular section of stream that I was fishing was full of fat little eastern brook trout with the odd resident brown trout that usually held a key piece of habitat that was its sole territory. The Brown trout in this upper area of the creek were smaller in length than those that inhabited the lower reaches of the creek but they were plenty fat and usually much more colorful than their downstream cousins.

Having fished this stretch of creek on numerous times previous, I had memorized all of the accessible spots along its course, where a fly fisher could get in a cast or two. On this outing I had decided to push the parameters of previous trips by trying to fish some new more difficult water that required a crouched approach thru thick willows. To access these new spots, I had to keep the rod pointed in the right direction, threading the tip through the willows in front of me as I maneuvered to the waters edge.

By rabbit tracking along the creek using this method of approach, thru the tangle of diamond willow and water birch, I would come to a likely looking pool or run where a trout may lie. Upstream of the chosen spot, I would feed line thru the guides of my fly rod and try to roll cast my short leader, fly, weight and strike indicator downstream of where I thought the trout were holding.

In most pools, hidden undercuts or runs, the trout didn't seem to mind that the fly was not drifting free with the current, the nymph that I was using must have just past as another food item, regardless of its motion. The trout that I hooked that day, hit the fly with great aggression. Most of them were small brook trout that I had trouble landing from my kneeling position in the brush.

When I hook a trout, I would reel in the line up to the indicator that was in a fixed position on my leader and then I would have to withdraw my rod so that I could grab onto the line and pull the small trout up to my hand for release at the waters edge. It was kind of an unorthodox method of landing a trout but it worked fine.

Further downstream I came to a longer deep run concealed beneath a canopy of mature willows. At the end of the run, the creek flow disappeared under a tangle of willow growth from both banks. A distinct foam line with floating debris had collected at the edge of the willow branches on the waters surface. I knew that there was a trout holding just below the cover, this kind of habitat is a perfect hold for trout, especially a larger fish.

From my position upstream, I repeated the process of feeding out line to allow my strike indicator as free a drift as possible. When the indicator hit the foam line in front of the surface cover it disappeared below the surface in a sudden plunge which indicated a take. I set the hook and found a large fish on the other end of my line. The trout made a screaming run downstream below overhanging willows and who knows what. I thought for sure that I was going to loose this fish, it was too big and the cover above the water and below would result in a tangle that I could not deal with from my position.

About 15 yards downstream, the trout finally stopped its initial run in a tangle of submerged willow. I could feel the trout on the end of my line but I could also feel the willow snag that the fish had got caught up in. I released some slack to the fish and it moved further downstream free of the tangle. During the next ten minutes or so, I played that trout in and out of submerged wood. Every time the trout caught my line in the brush, I would feed it some slack and some how managed to free it. It was like a tug of war between two opponents that were willing to give and take a little, as part of there strategy to win.

Eventually, the trout was worked upstream to a place where I could net it with my handy fold up net. It was a fine brown trout, about 15 inches long with beautiful coloration. After admiring the trout for a minute while reviving it, I released it back into its hidden environment. What a catch and what a battle, I was very lucky to have landed that- trout under those circumstances.

The Dogpound Creek is typical of many small spring creeks that are scattered across our province. Like many streams the upper reaches of a creek are difficult to fish with a fly rod, but the challenge is a major draw for some fly fishers. These typical small creeks are a great location for the spin fishing angler to fish, because of their large population of small trout and miles of water where they live. There were many times back in the 1980's when I left the fly rod at home and grabbed my spinning rod to join friends and family for a fun outing to fish for trout.

My fishing partners during these outings did not own fly rods but they were equipped with spinning outfits, so I felt compelled to enjoy the experience on the same level, which often resulted in some good catches of healthy brown and brook trout. This is the key to enjoying the sport of fishing, having fun and catching fish. Today I seldom use any fishing equipment other than the fly rods and reels that I own, but I cherish those past experiences where just catching fish and have a good time doing it was the goal.

Conservation

We all derive satisfaction from the sport of fishing in our own way, starting out in the sport in a simple but effective manner in my view is the best way to enter the sport. Young children are not born with a fly rod in their hands, and it may be some years before they are skilled enough in the basic mechanics of life. It will be years before they are able to comprehend the basic techniques involved in learning the use of a fly rod. In the mean time, it is my view that the best way to introduce them into the sport is to keep it simple and fun.

Maybe the first fish that they catch should be a keeper, they may want to keep it to show mom or dad or their friends, why deny them that opportunity. There will be plenty of time in their angling experience to learn about the importance of conservation, and this often starts by their observations of adults doing just that. I have noticed that children fishing the Mitford trout ponds in Cochrane have surprised me by their own choice to release trout that are stocked into the ponds on an annual basis.

These young kids can keep one trout each day if they wish, but I'm convinced that their observations of other adult anglers releasing their catch has influenced the younger generations desire to be just like the grown ups. When a catch and release policy is forced on young beginners right at the get go, they may reconsider what the purpose of fishing is really all about.

The use of fishing flies by beginners will provide the opportunity for them to catch their first fish, but also it will introduce them into a growing trend in the modern approach to fishing. This new age approach to fishing involves catch and release, selective harvest, an appreciation of the resource and the environment in which we practice the sport of fishing. If we are to preserve the sport of fishing into the future, we need to provide a friendly environment in which we can introduce a new generation.

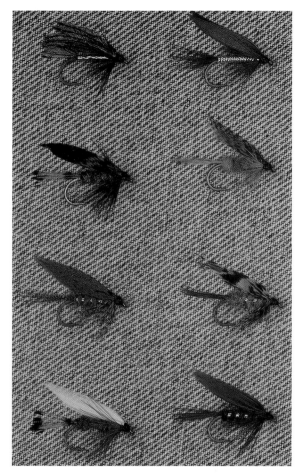

Part Three

Fishing Knots and Fly Patterns

In order to properly setup your fly, weight and bobber on the end of your line, you must have knowledge of some of the basic fishing knots to get the job done. There are dozens of different knots that one can use for tying line together or attaching the hook or lure. Every angler that has fished for any length of time has their own favorites, some are complicated and some are very easy to learn.

When I started fishing I learned by trial and error that knots are especially important when you have a fish on the end of your line. Over time, I picked up some good tips from more experienced anglers on what knots were best suited for setting up my line for fishing. After years of angling I now have a number of knots that I use confidently on my fly line, some of which I started using when I was young.

There are four basic fishing knots that I can recommend for beginners. The "Improved Clinch Knot" is the knot used to attach your line to the hook or lure, it is probably the most common knot used for this purpose by most anglers that I know. After some practice, the knot is easy to tie and has very good strength. Always remember to wet the line of the knot before you tighten it. Avoid using your teeth to clip off the tag end once the knot is completed, your dentist will back me up on this recommendation.

Secondly, "The Surgeons Knot" is a good choice for connecting two pieces of line together provided one length of the line is relatively short. If both lengths of line are long, you can use a "Blood Knot" to connect them. This third choice may take a little longer to tie, but it is the best and strongest knot that I know of for connecting two pieces of line.

Finally, tying loops is very important in setting up your fishing line. Loops can be used for connecting leaders on the end of your line and attaching a second fly in some cases. The easiest loop knot that I know of is the "Surgeon's Loop Knot". This knot is easy to tie and it is a strong knot when wetted properly for tightening.

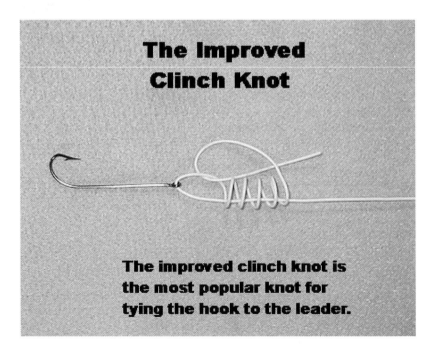

The Improved Clinch Knot

The improved clinch knot is the most popular knot for tying the hook to the leader.

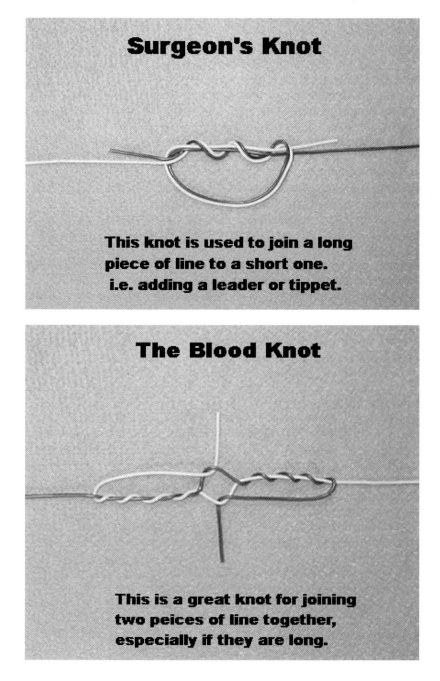

Surgeon's Knot

This knot is used to join a long piece of line to a short one. i.e. adding a leader or tippet.

The Blood Knot

This is a great knot for joining two peices of line together, especially if they are long.

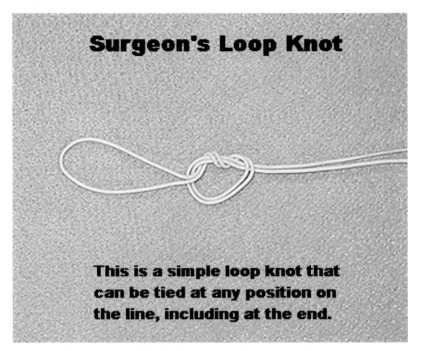

Surgeon's Loop Knot

This is a simple loop knot that can be tied at any position on the line, including at the end.

The use of leaders is an important bit of knowledge for fishing spooky trout. On the market today, there are spools of super thin and super strong monofilament that are available to the angler. This leader material is standard equipment for fly fishers. It is attached to the tip of the line in about 2 foot lengths and different pound test strengths for different applications, thus it is called "Tippet". For example, if you are fishing a standard 6.lb test monofilament and you would like a thinner less visible line at the end where you attach your fly, you can use a leader material.

When I'm fly fishing, I use a lot of tippet material. To reduce the time taken to replace the tippet on the end of my line, I use a loop to loop connection. This same method can be used on mono casting line. An advantage of the loop knot is noticed when you place a split shot up from the loop, the weight will not slide down the line to the fly when casting. If you decide to change from a nymph fly to a larger streamer, you can quickly change the tippet leader to a heavier test.

A loop to loop knot is very simple to achieve. You place the loop of the main line thru the leader loop and then you thread the end of the leader thru the main line loop. This can be accomplished when there is still a fly on the end of the leader. When you decide to change the leader, you push the loops into each other using both hands, and the loop to loop separates for detachment.

The loop to loop knot was a very important way of attaching leaders when I first started fishing. It is so easy and has so many applications.

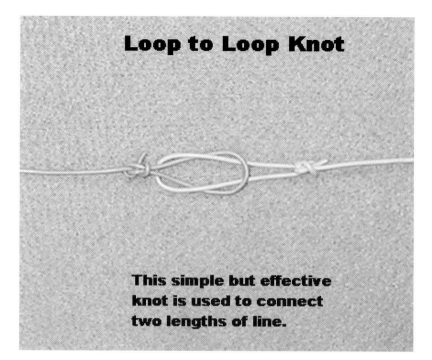

Loop to Loop Knot

This simple but effective knot is used to connect two lengths of line.

By concentrating on these four basic knots and the loop to loop connecting knot you can get started setting up for fishing the water. Practicing on the knots at home will speed up the process. You also have the option of pre-tying some of your flies with leaders before you head out for your fishing destination. The flies and leaders can be kept in a leader pouch or wallet.

If you are good at figuring out puzzles, well illustrated photos or drawings of fishing knots should come easy. In our age of internet access, there are some very good websites that show you how to tie the most popular knots used in the sport of fishing. Some sites have animation and others show sequence photo's with a slow speed option to let you see the knot tying progression.

The best way to learn most knots is to have an experienced tier show you the way. For some knots, there are simple short cuts that you can learn to achieve your goal. Hand and finger manipulation can make some of the most difficult knot tying a lot easier. The perfection loop is one of my favorite knots for creating a small loop knot on light leader. It wasn't until a master fly tier showed me a simple way of tying this knot that I started using it on a regular basis.

Here are some more knots that you can learn:
The Perfection loop, the Arbour knot for fastening the line to a reel spool and the Uni-Knot.

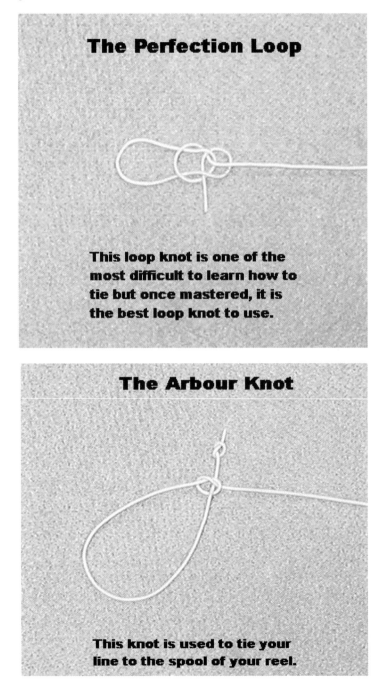

The Perfection Loop

This loop knot is one of the most difficult to learn how to tie but once mastered, it is the best loop knot to use.

The Arbour Knot

This knot is used to tie your line to the spool of your reel.

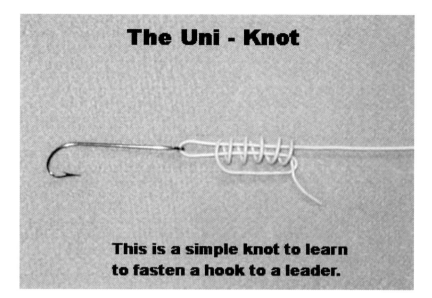

The Uni - Knot

This is a simple knot to learn to fasten a hook to a leader.

Fly Patterns

Once you have become competent in tying the basic knots necessary to setup your line with a fly, it will be time to acquire some artificial fly patterns to get started. I started tying flies over 20 years ago and in 1991 I began tying commercially for a gas station in Cochrane. Since that time I have also tied for two different fly shops. In the process I have learned a thing or two about popular fly patterns.

When you visit the local fly shop or sporting goods store you will be faced with deciding what type of flies you should purchase for your fishing trip. There are hundreds of patterns to pick and choose from and this can be a challenge for the novice. Over the years, I have learned from different fly fishers, both in the fly shops and on the water, their favorite patterns for most types of fly fishing. This usually boils down to about a dozen or so fly patterns that those anglers will make sure that they have in their fly boxes when they head out onto the water.

Before we examine some good starter fly patterns, let us take a minute to study some of the aquatic insect life that you are attempting to imitate. First we will begin with a brief summary of the life of an insect below the surface of the water. Insects go thru a number of different life stages to make it to adults. It is during these underwater stages and transitions that they become a target of feeding fish. Once they survive the initial adult stage of their life span, they mate and lay eggs to continue the species.

Depending on the type of insect, the number of life stages that they progress through varies. Caddis flies for example, go from egg to larva to pupa and then adult stages. May flies go thru the same number of life stages but their journey starts from egg to nymph to immature adult Dun (Sub-Imago stage) to mature adult (Imago stage) Spinner. It is during these different life stages after hatching from the egg that trout focus on in their feeding habits. It is by imitating nymph and larva fly patterns that copy these various life stages that we can attempt to fool trout and whitefish with our offering.

Streamers are used as a fly pattern that imitates small fish, leeches and other aquatic life that is larger and moves thru the water. These artificial flies are sometimes used as a first choice by fishers when it is larger fish that are being targeted. However, the streamer is a good alternative if your nymph and dry fly patterns are not producing results. They also require much more action to be effectively fished than other artificial fly patterns.

Traditional wet fly patterns are deemed to imitate insects, fish eggs and small fish. Some wet flies are called attractor patterns and they are supposed to simply entice sport fish into striking them out of curiosity. The fish has no hands to grab and examine something new and curious, their most effective part of their anatomy is their mouth, which is used too taste feel and reject. It is a fine line that separates what some anglers call streamers and wet flies, but some of the old classic wet flies still hold the title as traditional.

I have compiled a basic list of the most popular fly patterns that I have become familiar with and recommend for starting out, so that you will not be over whelmed by having to decide on your own when you walk thru the door of a retail store. Fly shops are also a great place to pickup info on some good basic fly patterns to get started. Further on in this book, I will mention other patterns that might be used for certain situations, but to start; let us look at the following selection:

Hare's Ear

Popular nymph fly patterns are tied to imitate specific aquatic nymphs, but there are a few that seem to cover a generalization of a number of different nymphs that fish feed on. At the top of my list is the Hare's Ear nymph. This is by far the most heavily used nymph pattern common among fly fishers thru out the country. The fly earned its name from the material that was used to tie it, the hair of a hare's ear, obtained from a snowshoe hare in its summer coat.

Since the introduction of the Hare's ear pattern, a number of variations have been added to the original design. The major modification involves the availability of various colors of the pattern. Hare's Ear nymphs can be fished on a dead drift, a stripping retrieve or just stationary. This is a must have pattern in your fly box.

Prince Nymph

The Prince nymph has been around for years, but recently it has become a main stay with many dedicated nymph fly fishers in the central east slopes region of Alberta. Originally called the forked tail nymph, it is said that the pattern imitates the water boatman and backswimmer beetles. In any case, the pattern is a hot item in many fly shops across the province. Fly fishers fish this imitation in a variety of sizes, usually in a short stripping retrieve, or a dead drift. The nymph comes tied in a bead head pattern, with a small brass bead tied in at the head or standard. The bead head pattern is preferred by many anglers because it does not require extra weight to sink.

Pheasant Tail

The Pheasant tail nymph is also an old timer in fishing circles. The name comes from the pheasant tail fibers that are used to tie the pattern. It is probably one of the most effective may fly imitations used in North America. Over the years a variety of variations have come along, one being the bead head pheasant tail which is a great pattern for getting down deep when you have to. The pattern is often fished on a slow retrieve or stripped in short or long pulls. It is common in most fly shops and you should carry a few especially for still water fishing.

Full Back Nymph

The full back and half back are also a main stay for fly fishers. Both of these patterns come in a wide range of variations are fished in still water and flowing streams. The name comes from the shell type back that is created by tying pheasant tail into a full or half back shell on the pattern. Between the two flies, a number of aquatic insects can be imitated. From beetles to mayflies, the full and half back are reputed to catch trout, grayling and whitefish through out the angling season.

Caddis Pupa

Caddis fly nymphs or pupa are often overlooked as effective fly patterns because of their unique no tail design, but they are a must. Especially during those super hatches when the trout are very selective about size and color. Since the introduction of the sparkle pupa imitation, fly fishers have gained considerable knowledge of how to fish the caddis pupa. Without a good selection of these in your fly collection, you may miss out on some good fishing.

The caddis pupa is taken by trout at all depths and in the surface film of the water. For under the surface, the deep sparkle pupa can be fished effectively in a short stripping retrieve or on a dead drift. This kind of nymph fishing fish a fly can be very frustrating for the novice, but it deserves some effort and you learn as you go.

When you do manage to connect with the right fly pattern, at the right time, fishing the caddis pattern patterns can reward you with some of the best fishing that you will experience. Caddis hatches can vary in size, with some hatches producing incredible amounts of food for trout, over a short period of time. This is when trout go into a feeding frenzy and the surface of trout laden water boils with fish. It is an amazing sight to witness and a fabulous time to fish.

Caddis fly patterns come in a large variety of sizes and colors. I have found that both olive green and tan in a size #14 are the most common choice for typical hatches on the water.

Chironomid (Midge Pupa)

This simple fly pattern is sometimes viewed as too sparsely dressed to attract a trout's attention. Nothing could be further from the truth! Chironomids are one of the most popular lake fly patterns that I know of. This is due to the fact that the majority of insect activity in lakes is the hatching of the midge pupa. With the huge volume of this insect present during feeding time, even large trout focus on the midge hatch.

I first read about chironomid fishing back in the 1980's. Lake fishermen from BC were "breaking ground" on this new fishing method and I was eager to learn. The trick with fishing the pattern, is too keep the fly stationary off the bottom or retrieve it in a very slow manor to imitate the pupa rising to the surface. You can also fish the fly right in the surface film, imitating an emerging insect that will take time to hatch into an adult fly.

I carry a wide selection of colors and sizes, with my two favorite colors being black and red. Patterns ranging from size 16 thru 10 tied on a long shank hook are common.

Shrimp

Another very common aquatic insect that is present in lakes and streams is the shrimp. There are a number of different kinds of shrimp but by far, the most common is the Gammarus or as some people call it "scud". Shrimp move in short spurts, propelled by their legs and abdomen. They will also stop and rest in a slightly curled position. I have had good luck fishing this pattern while retrieving the fly in short jerks or still fishing the fly suspended.

Depending on the lake, the best pattern colors are olive, green, brown and tan. I have found that the color of the lake bed can influence the color of the shrimp. Light colored marl lake beds usually have tan colored shrimp.

Where the lake bottom is covered with weeds, the most common color is olive/green or brown. The most common hook sizes are 10 and 12.

When I pull up to a new lake that I haven't fished before, I like to check out the shoreline to see what types of insects are present and active in the lake. This can be done by flipping over rocks, wood or other debris that is available just under the surface of the water. This is where you will find shrimp and identify their color and size.

For some experienced lake fly fisher's, the shrimp is the first pattern that they will fish when they start to cast a line. If there is no noticeable hatch happening, the shrimp pattern is a good starter fly. I like to fish shrimp patterns early in the spring and late in the fall on still water.

Stone Fly Nymph

One of my preferred nymph patterns throughout the year is the stone fly nymph. The stone fly will spend a number of years in the water before it migrates to the shoreline to reproduce. During its life span beneath the surface, the stone will go thru molting stages called instars as it grows in size. There is always a variety of small to large sized stone flies present in the stream bottom.

Stone flies inhabit the rocky bottom of fast flowing streams and are not present in still water. These invertebrates can grow to a very large size, which makes them a major target of big trout. Throughout the year, stone flies will lose their grip on the stream bottom and drift wiggling downstream to the jaws of a hungry trout or whitefish. This makes the stone fly a good pattern of choice what ever the time of year.

Right before the stone fly nymph is ready to leave the water for dry land, to hatch into an adult, the nymphs become very active. This movement and activity make the fly vulnerable to feeding trout. They can be dislodged from their hold on the rocks and drift downstream.

This is another case, were flipping a few rocks before you fish can be beneficial. I always like to do this on freestone streams before I choose a fly pattern. I like to find a relatively flat rock in moderate current and then I flip the rock over from the downstream side of the stone. This method is used so that any bugs underneath will not be flushed with the flow and I can get a clear look at them.

Wooly Bugger

When you arrive at your fishing destination and you are stuck on deciding what fly pattern to start with, or you start fishing a nymph and find that the fish are not taking your nymphs, it is time to try a little streamer fishing. By far, one of the most popular streamer patterns for trout water is the "Wooly Bugger". This pattern is a mainstay for most Bow River fishing guides when a streamer is considered.

The wooly bugger comes in a variety of colors, green, black, brown and white are some of the most popular. It can be purchased weighted or not weighted in many fly shops and retail outlets. In recent years a bead head version has ended up on the market, as well as those that are tied with brass bell eyes or cone heads. These weighted patterns allow an angler to fish the pattern without a split shot for weight. Buggers can be fished dead drift or stripped in short or long pulls at a variety of speeds. The pattern is very productive in both flowing and still water situations.

Leeches

The leech patterns that are sold in the market today vary in design; some anglers simply use a wooly bugger as an imitation. However, there are some great alternatives that you should try. One of my favorites is the rabbit strip leech pattern. The strip leech portrays a more slender silhouette than the bugger and I like the undulating action of the rabbit strip. This pattern can be fished slow or relatively fast, with short or long stripping of the line.

Marabough leech patterns and yarn leech patterns are also very popular among the fly fishing crowd. The key consideration when choosing a leech pattern is color and size. Black is the most popular color, with olive coming in at a close second place. In my experience, smaller patterns work the best early in the season and larger ones later on in the summer.

It seems that every fly fisherman has a different retrieve that they prefer when using a leech pattern. Short, fast or slow stripping motions or long slow pulls can produce results. I like to vary my method of working this pattern in the water. I have found that early and late season fishing requires a slower method for covering water. When the summer weather warms up the water, a faster action can be used with the pattern.

Western Coachman

The "Western Coachman" stream is a great white winged pattern with a design based on one of the most famous classic wet fly patterns know to fly fishers, the "Royal Coachman". The patterns long calf tail wing entices trout to strike the pattern with incredible enthusiasm. It has a reputation of producing catches of very large trout on many east slopes streams. You can fish this pattern in the same manor as all streamers, on the move.

I have used this pattern and ones that closely resemble it on some of my favorite brown trout streams. When the spring flows are high and turbid, the coachman pattern with its white wing will bring large trout in for the strike. If you fish this pattern under these conditions you will need enough weight to take the streamer deep, fast. Then start a jigging retrieve as soon as the pattern is near the bottom.

My preferred size of pattern is a size 8 with a size 10 for smaller streams and creeks. In high turbid flows, I like to fish a full winged pattern and in clear low flow conditions, a sparsely dress wing seems to perform better.

Muddler Minnow

Another famous streamer fly pattern is the "Muddler Minnow". This Canadian fly pattern was designed in the eastern part of the country to catch trophy sized eastern brook trout and it has become very popular out west over the years. It is said that the fly was tied to imitate a sculpin fish which is a prime food item for larger trout.

The Muddler is often fished deep in slow pulls or a steady retrieve, much the same way a sculpin swims along the bottom. Because the head of the Muddler minnow is tied with deer hair the fly is buoyant and you need a good amount of weight to get the pattern down to the bottom. For many anglers that fish this pattern, placing a split shot two feet up from the fly on the leader allows the pattern to suspend just off the bottom and be in the feeding zone for cruising or stationary trout. A few Muddler's in a variety of sizes is a complement to any fishers fly box.

The Marabou Muddler is a very popular version of this pattern and is used extensively on the Bow River. My of my old fishing buddies had a great winter day on the Bow using this pattern during one of our typical winter Chinooks.

Doc Spratley

The "Doc Spratley" streamer is a long time favorite in British Columbia lake fishing. The Spratley was originally designed for fishing for steelhead trout on the Fraser River in BC, but it was soon adopted by lake anglers across the province. Eventually the pattern ended up in fly shops and retail outlets in the province of Alberta and to the east and south.

I have fished the Doc Spratley on the Bow River for years and many other area streams as well. The pattern comes in a variety of colors and variations. Some of the most popular colors are black, green and red. My preferred method of fishing this pattern is to retrieve it in slow long pulls right off of the bottom.

In the 1980's I tied a Spratley pattern that combined the Spratley wing and incorporated the famous Royal Coachman body design. This version has become my own personal favorite in most fishing situations. I call the pattern the "Royal Spratley". I sell it in the fly shop that I tie flies for but I have not seen it else where yet. If you know a fly tier that can tie this pattern for you, it is worth a try.

There you have it! This is my basic list of patterns that should get you off to a good start. You will find that soon after you obtain these "first choice" fly patterns, your fly box will start to fill with many other well known and new fly patterns.

One of the main secrets to discovering a given pattern for fishing is to always watch the water. If you see a May fly hatch or a Caddis hatch on the water, try fishing a nymph of about the same size or larger. Nymphs are always larger than the adult on the surface. Until you learn how to correctly guest the size of the adult you may have to try your nymph patterns by trial and error.

Color is important in your selection of wet flies. In general, a dark grey or brown pattern is a good overall color to have on hand. Next most popular colors on the list are olive, green and tan. The problem with color choice is that there are a wide range of varying shades of color. It is because of this dilemma that my fly boxes are crammed with hundreds of patterns. This hording of flies is something that may not look forward to having to face in becoming a prepared fly angler, but it is a personal choice on how far you are willing to go in preparing yourself. On the other hand, I know of very competent fly fishers that carry only a few fly boxes and they always catch trout.

Pheasant Tail Nymph

Full Back Nymph

Caddis Pupa

**Chironomid
(Midge Pupa)**

Shrimp

Stone Fly

Wooly Bugger

Western Coachman

Doc Sprately

Blood Leech

Muddler Minnow

Hare's Ear Nymph

Prince Nymph

Pike and Walleye Streamers

Part Four

Reading Water and How You Fish It

It is one thing to be well equipped for fishing and it is another to know how and where to use that equipment. You have to hunt for your fish! Learning fish habitat, where they hide in cover, where they go to feed and simply where they hold or rest when they are not hiding or feeding. Combine the desire to learn all of these locations that fish inhabit, focus on them as your goal to understanding where fish live and then you will have a pretty good idea of what "Reading Water" means to the angler.

Accumulating knowledge of how to read water separates the novice from the seasoned angler. I have fished rivers and streams with more experienced anglers when I was a beginner and I marveled at how they could fish with the same fly, in the same area of water and catch so many more fish. It is often considered as "good luck" when you compare ones misfortune in catch rates. But luck is often not the case!

Those fishers that can consistently out fish you are most likely presenting their fly in the right spot in the current where they know the fish are waiting. A cast of only a foot too far or too short can make all the difference. Experienced fishing guides, like the professional Bow River guides, know this far better than most anglers. Years of fishing the Bow has trained them into knowing their water intimately, they know where the trout and whitefish hold and they direct their cliental to cast to them accordingly. They even give names to certain huge trout that hold in the same cover over the season.

This is one very important part of the angling experience that takes years to master, so you should not become frustrated. At this point in time all that you can do as a beginner is study some of the more identifiable holding water that is common on most rivers, streams and lakes. Over the years you will expand your knowledge and become a better angler as a result.

Flowing water habitats vary due to the different characteristics and flow dynamics of rivers, streams and creeks. There is a terminology that experienced anglers use to define the type of flowing water that they are fishing. Words like freestone, spring creek, glacier fed, silt laden, boulder strewn, meadow creek and canyon creek. Understanding these different kinds of water will help paint a picture of what you can expect when an angler describes a particular type of stream, river or creek. This is helpful information for preparation if you plan on trying the spot if it is recommended as a fishing destination.

Freestone Rivers and Streams

Freestone Rivers and streams are open channel waters that are susceptible to run off events that erode the stream banks and move bed materials such as gravel and boulders annually, thus the word freestone. This type of water is also known to be very productive in food production because of the quantity of loose bed material and woody debris that provides a good habitat for aquatic invertebrates. However, in order for the stream to be a good fishing stream it needs a supply of nutrient rich water to maintain the food cycle. Some high altitude mountain streams are not very productive trout waters because of the lack of nutrient in the water. If there are all of the right conditions for providing a good environment for trout, freestone streams are great places for the nymph and streamer angler.

If a stream is fed by a glacier, the water is often colored from the minerals of glacial till and the presence of high population numbers of trout is limited because of the lack of nutrient and aquatic invertebrates that are food for trout and mountain whitefish.

However, I have fish many a glacier stream with good success and an angler can be some what surprised by the voracious nature of the hungry trout that some of these streams and rivers hold. Bull trout and mountain whitefish seem to be particularly well adapted to inhabit these types of streams.

Spring Creeks

Spring creeks are quite the opposite of freestone or glacier fed streams. The spring creek is provided with an ample water supply from source springs that may be rich in nutrient. There are annual run off events but usually not enough to erode the stream banks to any degree, except to create undercuts and scour existing pools. With this relative stability of the stream banks and shore cover, the water is kept cool and clean with plenty of habitat for trout.

Due to the water clarity present in many spring creeks, they have a reputation of holding a population of very spooky trout. Many fly fishers consider spring creek fishing the ultimate challenge for presenting a fly without alerting the trout in the process. In the south central area of the province of Alberta, some of the better known spring creeks flow thru private land and access to their waters should be obtained by permission.

These flowing waters are reputed for their large populations of trout and are some of the best destinations for an angler that is up to the challenge.

There are spring- fed creeks in the foothills and mountains of the east slopes as well. Usually these creeks flow through forests of spruce and pine and in many valley bottoms thru meadows of bog birch and willow. Anglers call this type of creek a meadow creek and they often have a number of beaver dams that are targeted for the trout that live in these small impoundments.

Canyon Creeks

Where the creeks flow thru canyons of formation rock and boulders they are called canyon creeks. There are often plenty of pools and riffles on canyon creeks that hold resident trout and they are great places to cast a fly. The problem with some canyon creeks is the access to fish narrow rock cuts and steep cliff pools, as the angler is moving upstream. This is one of the few times that I will wear my chest waders while fishing a small creek. The waders allow an angler to cautiously wade up the canyon to fish areas that are normally not fished.

Canyon Creeks are usually found in combination with freestone streams in the mountain and foothills area of the east slopes. The canyon areas normally hole better pool habitats than the open freestone channels. This combination makes for an interesting outing if you can fish both types of water. The Waiparous Creek, Little Red Deer, Fallentimber to name just a few, all have good canyon areas to fish.

Boulder Strewn Streams

Rivers and streams that are vulnerable to very high run off events may have large boulders that are exposed in the channel. These large rocks provide pocket pools and riffle habitats for trout and they usually have plenty of gravel mixed in, which makes them productive habitats for the invertebrates in the food chain. Fishers refer to this type of water as boulder strewn and fishing it requires a lot of skill in order to identify the fish holding water. When you do spot a potential trout holding spot you will have to contend with a puzzle of conflicting currents that will affect the drift of your fly. The flow of the current has to be studied prior to your cast, so that you can present your fly properly.

One of my favorite boulder strewn streams that I love to fish is the Oldman River, on its middle to lower reach. I have fished this stream a number of times over the years and always look forward to the technical challenge of fishing its waters. With the Oldman's popularity, many anglers fish its waters but often overlook some of the prime pocket water habitat that is produced by the large rocks and sandstone outcropping present on the stream.

Low Gradient Streams and Rivers

Silt laden rivers and streams are flowing water bodies that have huge amounts of silt covering the bottom of the channel. This is usually the result of a moderate gradient in the channels course that allows silt to build up and smother the stream bed. There may be plenty of good fish habitats along the shoreline of this type of stream but the availability of food can be limited. Do not rule out a presence of trout in these kinds of waters, juvenile fish find this type of habitat a safe resort and larger fish that feed on them are attracted to this food supply.

Slow moderate stream channels with a quantity of silt produce good midge hatches for smaller fish and whitefish that prefer this food source. During certain times of the year larger fish may move into this kind of habitat to feed or to migrate for spawning. When faced with fishing slower moving water like this I like to start with a streamer pattern, fished tight into the bank. If it is a big river and the channel is large enough, a boat gives an angler good access to casting shoreline habitat.

If you launch a boat into this type of water, be sure to have both a bow and stern anchor in the boat to maintain stability in the channel for casting. Use a long line on the bow anchor and a short one on the stern anchor.

Part Five

Stream Hydrology, Habitat and How to Fish It

To start to learn about reading water, it is important to look at some of the basic rules of hydrology in flowing water. Current breaks caused by an obstruction or deflection of the flow and depressions in the streambed are just a few stream characteristics that we should investigate for starters. When you approach a shoreline on a river or stream, you have to have an understanding of some of the first water habitats that you should target.

Trout for example, do not like to expend energy unwisely; they prefer to find a nice comfortable break in the current that is located close to their source of food, with cover that they can retreat to, escaping any predators. One of the first identifiable habitats that most anglers look for is the pool. Pools are cause by structure or other influences that under high water conditions create a scouring effect that makes a deep depression in the bed of the stream. In streams with a soft bottom, the pool depth can be substantial.

The resulting depth of a pool gives fish have a place to hide and the flowing water entering a pool provides a smorgasbord of food items that enter the pool. Many of these food items are picked off at the head of the pool as soon as they enter it. However, the head of the pool is not the only feeding station for the trout that occupy it. There are other areas of the pool where the trout will hold and feed.

If the pool is located on only one side of the channel, there is an eddy line where the main current travels along the still water of the pool. This eddy line is another feeding lane for trout holding at the edge of the still water of the pool. The differential between the slow water of the pool and the main current is called the "seam line". However, because of its location in proximity to the near shoreline where the angler will be casting, it is a difficult piece of water to fish. The drag created by the still water on your line can limit the free drift of your fly.

Most pools have two areas that are know to fly fishers for their dry fly potential as well as being a good place to fish a nymph. One of the most important is the tail out of the pool. Trout and whitefish will often drop back from the main pool to hold in the "slick water" at the tail out of the pool. The relatively smooth surface of the tail out of a pool provides a good positional holding area for trout to see and feed on surface dry flies and emerging nymphs flowing with the current.

The other prime spot is the back eddy caused by the pool. A back eddy is typical of all pool hydraulics. When water flows over a deep pool the upwelling of the current at the end of the pool creates a back eddy that flows back upstream toward the head of the pool. Trout will face into this back eddy and pick up nymphs and dry flies that return with the flow. It seems unusual to find trout positioned in a downstream direction to feed on insects, but that is the reality of knowing stream hydraulics and how fish utilize these influences in their daily life habits.

Trout will ideally position themselves in the small area along the head of the eddy, where they can see food items coming into the pool and coming up from the back eddy. It is in this prime location that you will often find the larger fish of the pool holding at prime times, such as early morning and later on in the evening. With the trout holding in this pocket water so close to the shoreline, an angler has to be very careful when approaching the water not to spook the resident fish.

The more quiet areas of the pool are usually reserved for resting fish and are difficult to fish because of the conflicting currents caused by the seem line of the pool and the back eddy. Pools are great places to fish for trout and whitefish, but you have to devise a plan of how you will fish a pool prior to approaching it.

Feeding fish locate themselves at the head of a pool where food enters from the shallower flowing current from upstream. The trout and whitefish will position in a location that will allow them the first opportunity at what ever insects come to their feeding station. Anglers can successfully fool these feeders by presenting a fly in the shallow run that flows over the drop off on the upstream side of the pool.

Using a slip bobber adjusted to the correct depth of the shallow run upstream of the feeding zone, you can cast well upstream of the pool, allowing your fly and weight to sink to the right depth before the fly drifts over the drop off. The same method can be used for fishing the tail out and the back eddy line. If the trout are taking surface dry flies at the tail out or in the eddy, you can fish your fly up from the bottom, where the trout are suspended in the water taking nymphs and dries.

If there is no surface action, you will probably have to present your fly just off the bottom. Remember that any takes on a wet fly without bait are short quick hits and you have to set your hook fast on any stops or dips in the floats drift. By minor adjustments in the location of the bobber stop on your line you can find the appropriate depth at which you should fish your fly.

You may want to consider fishing a nymph without a slip bobber when fishing the different areas of a pool. By using the right size split shot you can get your fly down to where the fish are and if the weight is the right size for the current it will bounce off the rocks on the bottom without snagging. With a light split shot, you will require light line to get a descent cast. Remember to keep your rod tip elevated and at the end of the drift you can retrieve the nymph using short or long jigging action on your rod tip as you reel in.

A streamer may also be considered for a fly pattern choice. A good place to start fishing a pool is at the top of the eddy, but do not stand at the top of the eddy when you start fishing it. If you walk up to the top of an eddy before fishing it properly, you may scare some fish holding at the top end. The best approach to start your casting at the top end of an eddy is to stand well upstream of the eddy and cast out and across the main current. When your fly swings into the seam line of the eddy, downstream from your position, you can start your retrieve back upstream.

Sport fish in flowing waters always face into the current. Approaching any likely looking water from an upstream direction will spook any fish that can see you coming. That is why it is a good strategy to cast to downstream holding water from a distance before you move down to the next potential holding water. If you are fishing a nymph as you travel upstream, you are in a better position not to have the prey see you approach. Fish have conical vision that allows them to see an area above, to their side and straight ahead, which leaves a blind area behind the fish.

I have spoken of eddies in fishing a pool, but shallow or moderately deep eddies themselves are probably one of the more common types of habitat that sport fish hold in. When you approach the shoreline of a stream or river you should first pick out the prominent eddies that occur on both stream banks. The eddy lines will be created by rocks or woody debris along the shoreline or a change in the channels direction, usually on the inside of a bend in the channel. This structure may influence the scouring of a pocket pool or deep run created by spring high water events.

The ideal direction in which you should approach to fish an eddy for drift fishing is traveling upstream, or as mentioned before, traveling downstream if you are streamer fishing or stripping in a nymph or other wet fly.

Eddies are probably the most common holding water that trout and whitefish frequent, because of the number of them that exist on most flowing streams. Fish prefer the quieter water of habitats that are located close to shore.

These habitats provide the free drifting food that is available in the main current and also any terrestrial insects that might happen to fallen into the water, like ants, beetles, grasshoppers and so on. If the current in the stream channel is moderate, fish will often hold further out into the main stem of the channel, out from the eddy seam line.

The nice thing about fishing eddies is the ease with which you can guess the depth for adjusting your slip bobber. Most eddy runs are fairly consistent in depth and provide a long drift of your fly at a given depth. If the eddy has been created by woody debris out from the bank, trout will often hold close to that cover or even in it. When you drift your fly close into the cover, the trout holding in the wood will sometimes dart out and take your fly.

You should fish a streamer or moving nymph pattern the same way you would in a pool. Start from a position upstream of the top of the eddy and cast out into the main current, when the fly swings into the seam line of the eddy you can begin your retrieve. If the eddy is a large one such as those found on big water, you can move downstream as you fish, casting out and across the seam line and jigging in as you reel. Trout will often take the streamer or nymph as it swings into the seam line.

There are other types of holding habitat that you should watch for on medium to small sized streams. One of my favorite spots is an undercut bank, usually located on the outside bend of the channel. Trout love undercuts, they provide overhead cover and a location close to the main current where food is on the drift. These prime holding habitats are often home to some of the streams larger trout.

Fishing a nymph with a slip bobber from a downstream position, you must present the fly well upstream of the target area so that you don't spook the fish. If the undercut is on the outside of the channel, the current will maintain your bobber and fly close to the bank on its drift. Where the current flows directly into the bank creating an undercut, you need to cast into that current and when your bobber floats into the bank, you must reel in or hold the rod tip up to prevent the bobber and fly from slipping under the bank. This measure will keep the bobber tight alone the bank as it continues on its drift thru the run.

For streamer casting, you can cast out from the bank from an upstream position and let your streamer swing into an area close to the bank for the retrieve. If the streamer swings in too close into the bank, position your rod tip pointing across the channel to keep the streamer from snagging on the bank. Make sure to have the right weight to get the streamer down to the bottom or below the undercut.

Another method of fishing a nymph or streamer in an undercut is called "dapping". This technique is used by dry fly fishers to lure trout out of holds where a cast from a fly rod is either too difficult or impossible. The dapping technique can be used with a wet fly as well. By standing over an undercut or just upstream, you can drop a fly with a weight into a habitat and jig it or wiggle your rod tip to impart a lively action to your fly.

A recent experience comes to my mind when I think of occasions when I have successfully used the dapping technique to fool a trout. I was fishing the Little Red Deer River with an angling buddy of mine and we had just spent the day fishing a reach of the Little Red upstream of the truck. It had been a great day and both of us had caught some nice brown trout. We were headed back downstream at a faster than normal pace to cover some ground before dark.

I had a tandem nymph set up on my fly rod, with a small foam strike indicator about 5 feet up from the upper nymph. As I was walking the heavily forested bank of a large beaver dam I came to a large downed spruce tree that had fallen into the deep water next to the bank. The thick rooted base of the tree provided what I thought to be an ideal habitat for a large brown trout. However, because of the thick cover of willow and other spruce trees there was no way to cast to the likely hold with my fly rod, from a distance.

The only viable option was to fish my nymphs from a spot directly over the downstream side of the tree trunk. The water was very deep below the bank and it appeared that there was an undercut below the root ball of the tree, which was still attached to the bank. I started to fish the spot by dipping my lead fly into the water about 6 inches out from the bank. When the fly had sunk to about two feet, I started to wiggle the rod tip to give the fly some movement.

I had just started the action on the fly when out from under the bank darted a 16 inch brown trout. The trout gulped the fly and immediately returned towards its cover beneath the bank, I set the hook. The surprise of that trout taking my fly in such an instant prompted quite a victory yell that broke the silence of the evening. Minutes later, with some degree of difficulty, I managed to lie down on the bank and with arm extended, reach my net down to the battle weary brown. It was a perfect finish to an already great day on the water!

Pocket Water

There are other habitats that need to be identified on flowing water streams and rivers. I have previously mentioned the expression "pocket water" when describing fishing boulder strewn water and how this type of water provides plenty of pocket water. Pocket water is often discussed by experienced stream anglers while in conversation about their past fishing exploits.

Fishing this kind of fish holding habitat deserves a few paragraphs of description in it's self. The title refers to a small type of habitat present on most trout streams. Pocket water can be described as any little habitat where trout and whitefish may be present, other than those habitats that are the main focus of most anglers. These habitats are often overlooked primarily due to their size.

A pocket may be a small depression in the streambed with adequate flow entering or passing over it. It could be a small bit of shaded cover under a rock or log that is noticeable only to the trained eye of an experienced angler. Small pools that are caused by erosion or in the stream channel may be located in shallow riffles or quiet runs where the current is moderate and the surface is slick with little disturbance.

Some pocket water is created during the early spring ice flows on a stream or the high water run-offs that occur shortly after. A good place to look for small pocket pools is on the upstream side of large boulders in rivers and streams. When spring ice collects on the upstream side of these boulders it is tipped up on its side by the force of the current and in the process can excavate a depression in the streambed just up from the rock.

These depressions can also occur on a major scale on streams and rivers when ice dams are formed during ice breakup. I have know Bow River guides that make an early season drift on the lower Bow River prior to spring run-off, just to identify some of these ice caused pocket pools that will be invisible to the eye later on when the river levels are higher. The guide's memory of these sweet spots helps them with their daily catch rates when clients come to fish.

The Bow River is known to weed up late in the season when the water levels drop a bit and the growth of large-sheath pondweed starts to blanket the shallower runs. As a result, where there are moderate flows, these areas produce ideal conditions for the weed to grow thick and it can become a real problem for the angler. In these runs there are small pockets of weed free water where large trout love to hold. The only problem with fishing these areas is when you catch a fish and you have to contend with the trout's ability to tangle you up in the weeds. However, this is considered pocket water and it deserves to be fished regardless of the consequences.

Gravel Bars

Rivers and streams are dynamic systems that are continuously changing. Having fished many area streams over the years I have witnessed some of the change that has occurred. The direction of a river or streams course will change over time. High water events, the movement of spring ice and the influence of bank erosion can alter the direction of the stream channel. The streambed is affected by these subtle changes and bed materials are continuously on the move from year to year.

One of the most noticeable changes that I have seen on the Bow River is the reformation of gravel bars as they slowly move downstream, having new small gravel added to them every season when a substantial run-off has occurred. On the edge of these bars, whether they are located along one shoreline, downstream of an island or across the entire river, trout and whitefish will stack up on the downstream side. These areas could be considered pools but in many cases they are just hidden drop offs on long runs.

Fishing the drop offs is usually a good bet for hungry trout or mountain whitefish. The fish have a preference for hold right at the drop and picking up any food item as it passes from the shallower water upstream over the edge of the bar. During feeding prime time, the fish will sometimes move up onto the shallow water upstream to feed, in any case, these gravel bars are definitely a good place to cast a fly

If you adjust your slip bobber to the depth of the streambed up from the drop off, you should be in business. Casting a streamer so that it skirts the edge of the drop will often produce some mighty hard hits form trout that are a custom to competing with some aggressive neighbors. Don't rule out a cast or two over the run upstream of the drop during prime feeding time either.

I was fishing one such gravel bar on the lower Bow River last year with a river guide friend and his father in law. The bar that we were fishing spanned the entire river at a bend upstream of a high clay bank. We had stop to fish the spot across the channel from the high bank where the gravel bar came to a weed bed on the shoreline. I decided to fish the nymph set up that I had on my fly rod while my guide friend was convinced that the streamer on his rod would produce a trout.

I waded in to fish the drop off and my friend moved upstream into the shallower run up from the drop off. I was first to hook a good rainbow of about 18 inches as my fly drifted over the drop, close to shore. After working the trout through the weeds along the slack water in front of me I managed to tail the trout and release it. No sooner than I had released my trout that I heard a huge splash and a yell "Who-o-o-a". I looked up in time to see a large rainbow trout take a second jump, high out of the water and the scream of a fly reel drag as the trout made a run for the middle of the river.

My friendly guide had hooked the large trout on a streamer stripped across the shallow run. After a few minutes of fight, the tired rainbow gave in and we both admired the 24 inch rainbow trout before it was let free to fight again. It had been a relatively slow day for the Bow River, but hooking both nice rainbows in a matter of minutes was a great enthusiasm booster for all three of us.

Riffles and Runs

Riffles and runs are prime fish holding habitat. These two types of fish habitat are by far the most productive for the nymph fisher. Trout and whitefish that are present in moving water are opportunists and are more likely to take an offering than those fish holding in many other types of habitat. The speed with which the food passes them often leaves little time for the fish to have second thoughts about eating or letting the food pass by. This is probably why I have always had some of my best angling in both these types of water.

A riffle is a section of flowing water that is broken up by the roughness of the stream bottom, which in most cases consists of rubble and small boulders. These rough bed materials cause the surface of the water to be broken into small sized wavelets and conflicting currents. The disturbance in the surface creates a break in the current and some cover for holding trout and whitefish if there is adequate depth present.

A run is a stretch of flowing water that is on the move and has sufficient depth for hold fish. It too is often made up of a rocky bottom, but has enough depth that the surface is relatively smooth. The depth of a run is usually fairly consistent throughout its duration, but there may be areas that drop to a deeper depth. Stream and river runs are often created by a constriction in the channel width or they may be located on the outside of a bend in the stream.

One of the most promising features of runs is their length and the opportunity to fish a run can provide an angler with a chance of catching more than a few fish out of one relatively short section the stream or river channel. I prefer to fish runs from a downstream position, fishing upstream as I go. If you catch a trout at the bottom of a run, there is less chance that you will spook any trout that are holding further upstream, provided that you keep the fighting fish from moving upstream during the battle. Riffles can produce similar results if they are long enough, but in most cases they are short in length.

For the slip bobber angler, adjusting the bobber stop is the secret to success in fishing riffles and runs. If you guess the right depth you are probably in for some good action. Casting upstream and reeling in as your bobber drifts down current will work the best. Streamers can be fished from an upstream position and are cast out and across the current with an immediate retrieve using a long or short jigging action.

Small Creeks

Throughout the east slopes of the Rockies there are a number of small mountain creeks that feed into the rivers and streams that many of us are familiar with. Many of these small creeks are great trout waters that support populations of smaller sized trout such as brook trout, cutthroat trout, rainbow trout, bull trout and brown trout. These small creeks can support good trout populations without attracting too much attention from most anglers, but what a gold mine for those of us that enjoy fishing these small jewels.

The headwater areas of many small creeks are less susceptible to the high water events that occur on larger streams and rivers, as a result the shore cover and bank stability allows trout to inhabit areas that trout on larger water would not consider. With good shoreline cover and an overhead canopy of willow and trees, trout feel safer in their environment and will hold in areas that you would normally pass by.

Slow moderate flows thru featureless channels in small creeks can be home to the resident trout. It is with this in mind that I try not to pass by any likely looking water bye on small creeks. The old saying, said by many a long time fisher, is that you don't know what you have missed until you pass it by. The basic meaning behind this saying is that if you pass up a piece of water when you're fishing, you will not realize your error until you walk up to it and see the trout you missed spook and dart for cover.

The creek that you are fishing may be small but the need to stay back from the target area of your fly presentation is important. If the channel is narrow or the wind is blowing, a good cast may be hard to achieve, so try and use the current to your advantage by drifting a slip bobber and fly down to the trout. Short underhand casts are very effective and easy if you take some slack line in your free hand and release it on an underhand cast or flip cast.

The dapping of a fly can be especially useful on small creeks, but you have to approach the spot that you are going to fish with stealth. Fish can pick up on any vibrations emitted from the bank, such as foot steps, so step lightly. It is always a good idea to stay back away from the bank if you can. If you glare down at a potential holding area of trout, chances are that they will see you before you see them.

Beaver Dams

Beaver dams on small creeks are a totally different environment to fish than that of flowing water, rivers and streams. On some small creeks the beaver dam is the only viable option for the angler, especially during late season low water conditions. The type of aquatic insect life that inhabits beaver dams is different in general than the flowing water food chain so the flies that an angler uses can be classified as still water patterns. On flowing water you can flip a few submerged rocks along the edge of the water and examine the invertebrates that are present. On still water, determining what bugs are present is a different story.

When it comes to reading water, still water habitat is far more difficult to read than flowing water. However, there are some bits of knowledge that I have learned over the years that will help you in understanding what to look for when you angle still water lakes, reservoirs, ponds and beaver dams. Let us start with beaver dams on smaller streams and creeks.

There are small beaver dams and large. The smaller dams are generally easier to fish than the larger dams because of the narrow channel area that is dammed. Large dams can be a puzzling when you are first faced with deciding where to start fishing. One of the most challenging tasks is trying to determine where the submerged creek channel is in a large flooded area. It is often in these deeper channels that trout will hold and cruise for insects; sometimes they will leave the deeper channel and travel the shallows and the shore line grass and sedges looking for a meal.

Large dams will follow the lay of the land and in many cases the depression created by years of water erosion. There is usually a slight meander to even larger beaver dams, and it is with this in mind that you can pretty much guess where the submerged channel might be. Look at the bank contour and height along the shoreline of the dam. This will help you find the outside edge of the bends in the submerged channel. A set of polarized sun glasses is a handy tool for helping an angler to read water and still water is no exception. The glasses will cut the glare on the surface of the water and help you see into the depths.

At different locations on a big dam there are beaver runs that are excavated back into the shoreline to provide access to feeding areas for beavers. Trout love to hold in the deeper water of the beaver runs near the shoreline and out into the channel. The beavers dig these runs in a straight line from the deep water to the shore, so you can use the alignment of the runs as a guide to where they go in the main channel. Casting a fly into one of these runs will sometimes produce the larger trout present in the dam.

At the upstream end of the flooded area of the dam, where the creek channel enters, is almost always a good location to catch trout. Trout that are fond of feeding on flowing water insect life prefer the inflow area of the dam for the free drifting insects that are present and easily taken for food.

The fresh oxygen rich water that enters the inflow area is also sought after by trout.

The deep water area just upstream of a beaver dam is a good place to find trout on larger dams. This location on a dam site is usually the deepest part of a large dam. Beavers are constantly pushing mud from the channel up onto the dam to seal leaks and fortify the existing dam. This creates a deep pool that is maintained on a regular basis. Trout will often hold in this deeper pocket, especially on bright sunny days when the comfort of a cool deep pool provides security.

There are two basic approaches to fishing a beaver dam, be it large or small. Casting a streamer or nymph with a split shot for an active retrieve or the dead drift of a nymph below a slip bobber. Beaver dams usually are full of snags so working a moving fly at a given depth may result in a few lost flies, but that goes with the territory. The technique of swimming a streamer thru the depths can result a very productive outing.

Small minnows will often retreat to, or hold in the shelter of shallow semi-submerged shoreline grass, this type of cover is usually located in the top end of beaver runs or low lying flooded areas. With this in mind, presenting a streamer close to these habitats will sometimes be very effective. When you cast your fly into the shallows you must start your retrieve immediately so you don't snag on the bottom. Long or short jigging on your retrieve will give the fly the desired action to imitate a minnow, leech or swimming nymph.

For nymph fishing the channel, a slip bobber adjusted to the right depth can be cast upstream and left to complete a slow drift downstream with the minimal current. Sometimes an occasional jerk of the bobber and fly will insight a take on your fly. If there is no current to move your fly, just sit tight and wait for a slight tug on the bobber. Again, I have to stress the importance of being ready to strike at the instant that your bobber dips. These trout are sometimes curious and will just sample the fly for an instant.

When the trout are cruising for nymphs that are a prime target, and your imitation is close enough to the natural, the hit can be substantial, which buy's you a bit of time in your response. A good case in point is when the trout are feeding on midge pupa or chironomid's. When trout are moving for these smaller aquatic insects, they will not stop for a take, but rather continue swimming as they swallow the pupa. This makes for some good action for the angler.

On some occasions a very slow retrieve is required to imitate a small nymph. If this is the case, an angler can remove the split shot and the slip bobber set up and slowly reel in an un-weighted nymph with a fixed bobber attached to the line, about four feet up from the fly. You can purchase bobbers that will attach to your line in a fixed position and that are stream lined enough to create little resistance when reeled in at a slow speed. Slip bobbers can also be jammed onto the line in a fixed position, using a small piece of a tooth pick.

Fishing beaver dams is great fun and especially good for groups of more that one angler. Small streams or creeks are often too small an angling destination for more than two anglers, the traffic created by more than one angler on small water can alert the resident trout population and cause them to retreat to any available cover. Beaver dams on the other hand, can be fished by a number of anglers without stressing or alerting the resident trout population. Just remember to remind everyone involved to approach the water with a degree of caution, so they do not disturb the fish.

When I think of some of the more memorable outings that I have enjoyed fishing beaver dams in recent time, I think of a fishing trip that an angling buddy and I enjoyed on Sibbald Creek a few years ago. The reason this particular trip stands out in my mind compared to other trips to this creek is the number and size of trout that we both caught on that day that we fished the stream.

Sibbald Creek is a rather small creek in nature but because of the number of large and medium beaver dams on the creek and the brook trout that inhabit its waters, it is a great place to cast a fly with friends on a mild summer's day or for that matter any summer day. You can spend hours fishing a short reach of beaver dams without wearing your legs out sloughing thru the willows of a small creek channel.

On this particular day my fishing buddy Troy and I had been doing well catching lots of brook trout with the landing of a few very large trout that had not been harvested for the frying pan in previous years. I had fished my way downstream of Troy to large beaver dam that promise to hold some good trout.

For this reach of creek I had changed my fly to a white winged streamer pattern with a BB size split shot about 2 feet up from the fly pattern. The streamer pattern was chosen so that I could cover the big water of the dam with a series of casts to the far shoreline grasses. I was hoping that my fly would closely imitate one of a population of small minnows that were hiding in the shallow flooded grasses and beaver runs on the dam.

As I worked my way down the channel of the beaver dam, I came to a wide piece of water just upstream from a small island of high ground about the size of an old beaver lodge. It may well have been an old lodge but years of growth had made it into a hump of grass about 3 meters across and a few feet above the flooded water line. On the far shore line was a bank of water sedge that dropped off into deep water. There was an old diamond willow stump that tipped from the bank into the darker water along the drop off.

The upstream side of this piece of old willow would be a good spot to cast too for starters, so I managed to drop my fly tight to the grass just up from the stump. I let the fly sink down for a second and then started a retrieve with long slow pulls. On the second strip of the line, I felt a solid hit that I knew instantly was not a snag. I set the hook and was immediately confident that I was into a large trout, but it seemed too big to be a typical brook trout for this creek.

The line where it enters the water is always what you watch when your into a nice trout in a beaver dam. It is necessary to steer your fish away from any submerged wood or shoreline grass when you are trying to land the fish. There was a single old willow limb coming up from the bottom of the channel in front of me and I was attempting to play the trout on the near side of the channel as it milled about back forth just downstream.

There are huge sucker fish in these waters and by the strength of this fish I wondered briefly if that was what was on the end of my line, but I was fishing a streamer and I had never caught a sucker on a streamer before. The fish was fighting like a large trout, indicated by the head shakes and quick short runs. My curiosity was further heightened a few seconds later when I saw the trout's flashing side in the depths as it maneuvered just a rod length away. It was definitely not a brook trout and it appeared to be stocky and light in color. Could it be one of the rare bull trout that had once dominated these waters?

By that time I had already yelled to Troy that I had a monster on my line. I could see Troy walking downstream toward me at a quick pace. As the trout turned back upstream and swam in front of me, it again flashed its colors. This time I could hardly believe my eyes! I once again shouted to Troy "I think I have a rainbow trout on – and it's about 26 inches long". It was at that point in time I knew I had better land this trout or my fishing partner is going to think that I'm full of it!

It might have been my momentary lapse in concentration, or maybe not but I allowed the trout to turn back downstream and wrap my line around the single willow limb that I had spotted earlier. The trout, feeling the resistance of the line on the snag decided it was time to change direction and in an instant the trout was free of my fly. Maybe this sudden turn of fate explains why the rainbow had grown to such a large size.

I looked back upstream at Troy, who was about 60 meters away, as I exclaimed "I lost him – he wrapped me around a willow". Troy went back to fishing and I moved downstream to cast my fly in new water. If only I could have landed that trout or at least held it long enough for my fishing buddy to see my prize catch still in battle, oh well, that's fishing!

The fact that I knew there was a large rainbow trout in these waters had me puzzled. Did the trout migrate upstream from the Jumpingpoung Creek some how? The Sibbald Creek was a tributary, but there were all those beaver dams to get past. There is a man made pond a few kilometers upstream, at the headwaters of Sibbald Creek that is stocked annually with rainbow trout; the fish must have been a wash down from a previous stocking I thought.

As I fished downstream to the next beaver dam, I could not stop thinking about the trout and the puzzle of where it came from. Then my trend of thought was suddenly interrupted by the yell from upstream. Troy had hooked into a big one! As is always the case when your fishing buddies hook into large fish, you head straight for them, and if you're real smart, you don't leave your camera at home!

When I got back up to where Troy was, he was still fighting the trout. I could tell immediately by the delicate manor in which he was playing the trout that he was very concerned about loosing it, something that I had neglected to do 30 minutes earlier. I waded out to Troy's side and by then the large rainbow trout was near the shore sedge in front of him. It was a big fat beautiful rainbow trout with magnificent color. Troy had hooked the fish on a leech pattern just upstream of where I had battled mine.

The trout was finally steered into the bent down sedge and shallow water at our feet. I measured the rainbow at 24 inches and guessed its weight at about 6.lbs. I was very disappointed for Troy's sake that I had forgotten my camera. In any case we admired the trout for a brief period of time and then safely released it back into the channel. I was really happy with the catch, because now the story of my big trout had some merit.

Lakes

The eastern slopes of the Rockies in the south central area, does not have what we can consider a great lake fishery for trout. Apart from the prairie pothole lakes to the east and the high mountain lakes in the Rockies, the still water fishing opportunities do not draw much attention. Many of us will travel north in the Province or into British Columbia to fish the many rainbow and brook trout lakes.

Still water fishing is a totally different experience for the angler and the ability to read still water in comparison to flowing waters requires a different set of guidelines. The techniques used are based on knowledge acquired and passed on by experienced lake fishers, many of them that are residents of BC's lake districts. Once you have learned a little about the best approach to fishing still waters, you are in for an interesting angling experience that will open new doors for your fishing enjoyment. This new found knowledge will change the way in which you look at a lake, pond or reservoir.

When I first fished lakes with a fly, I felt a little intimidated by the vast area of water in which I had to choose a spot in to fish. I knew instinctively that trying an area close to shore near a drop off was a practical start, but I didn't have a clue about how to read water in such a setting. Over time I picked up bits of knowledge from reading books on lake fly fishing and tips from other fly fishers that I had the good fortune to meet and receive advice from. Eventually, I began to understand the environment of lakes better and some of the intimidating immensity of it all, started to disappear over time.

There are certain common traits that an angler can look for when deciding where to fish and what to fish on lakes, ponds and reservoirs. The first being whether or not there is an inflow or outflow on the lake. On reservoirs the inflow is a given, usually a stream or river and the outflow is a dam. Where ever there is in flowing streams or creeks on a lake, you can count on the presence of feeding fish but the size of such stream and where they are located may require some research.

Lake fish are cruisers when they feed, out of necessity they have to travel to collect a meal. On flowing rivers and streams, fish can hold and wait for their diner to arrive. This is not the case in lakes, unless there is an inflowing stream that will provide them with an environment similar to flowing water. Fish are opportunists, if they can hold in a particular habitat that makes life easier for them; they will collect there in numbers. Where flowing streams and creeks enter lakes there is such an environment.

Unless you are in a boat that is positioned just offshore, drifting a nymph down the current of an inflowing stream into a lake is a difficult task. You can cast out into the in coming current from shore using a slip bobber and then feed line off of your reel as the bobber travels out into the lake. If you try this method you must take care not to allow too much slack in your line as the float moves with the flow, if you need to set the hook, a tight line is necessary.

From a boat, anchored along or in the middle of the inflow, drifting a slip bobber will be more effective and easier to control. The depth adjustment should be made to present your fly along the bottom of the incoming channel, so that it slips over the drop off where most trout will be positioned. If the lake bed out from the drop off isn't too deep, you can readjust the bobber stop to place your fly near the bottom.

If you have no choice, other than to be fishing off of the shore, a streamer or moving nymph with a split shot will get you out and across the in flowing water or along the seam line. Make sure that you let your fly sink to a good depth before you start your retrieve. If you can cast across and upstream of the drop off, stripping or jigging your pattern along its edge is a great method for enticing active fish.

Out flows on lakes is a different environment to fish. Trout will position themselves right in an area where the current starts to draw the lake water in a slick surface flow. The circumstances for trout to be holding in such an area is the same as for in flowing streams. The fish can find a position or hold that will allow them to take a meal as it flows over or by them. In this out flow location, nymphs or emerging nymphs are a good choice. Imitations of these can be fished on a slip bobber with a weighted nymph or fixed bobber and nymph without a weight. Fishing a streamer or a moving nymph will require a faster retrieve with the current or fished up and across the flow.

For the main body of a lake, an angler has to assess the shoreline features and submerged structure to help find trout. The standard shoreline features that are commonly identified as good locations to fish are points of land that disappear into the depths, shallow bars and bays with prominent drop offs. In the lake bottom there may be humps of submerged lake bed that is close to the surface or weed beds along the drop off. Weed beds are a valuable habitat in lakes and they may be present in bays or on points and bars. The weed bed is a prime aquatic insect habitat that in turn attracts fish.

All of these areas help the angler analyze where to start fishing on a lake or reservoir. The time of day in which you are fishing is also an important part of the puzzle. Early morning and late afternoon into evening is the standard feeding time for trout and other fish. During that time period fish will be present in the prime habitats that I have previously mentioned, to search for food. Later in the morning, the trout may retreat to the safety of the deep cool water of the lake to rest, until later in the day when they once again have feeding on their mind.

One of the first things that I look for when I look over the shore area of a fishing lake is if there is any surface feeding activity. A pair of binoculars is a handy tool for this inspection. Even if there is no major insect hatch occurring, trout will often give away their presence by rising to the surface to take something of interest. If this sign of trout is observed then I will immediately head for the spot where I have seen the rising trout. We have to remember that trout feed on sub-surface insects 90% of the time, so any indication of a few trout on the surface can be seen as just a portion of the population that is present below the water in a given area.

There are a number of techniques used to fish the still water of a lake. Much of what you are trying to imitate will be submerged and some guess work is necessary to find a fly pattern that will do the job. A number of the nymph and streamer patterns that are used in streams and rivers can also be used in still water. Lakes have good populations of May flies, caddis flies, beetles, midge's, leeches and small minnows. However, the habitats of these aquatic insects and forage fish will differ slightly from those that are found in flowing water.

There are swimming nymphs and pupas present in lakes, as well as the slower moving crawling invertebrates that are also very common in quiet water. I have found that some patterns can be fished dead still and produce good results. Midge pupa is a great example of such a pattern that is commonly fished stationary or with very little movement. The pupa of the midge is referred to in most species as a chironomid. From its transformation from larva to pupa on the bottom of a lake, the insect begins a slow accent to the surface of a lake by expelling gases in its body. It is during this slow accent to the top of the water that trout will feed veraciously on this little bug.

When trout are after midge pupa, you can see them in the shallower areas of a lake darting about taking the pupa in a steady frenzy. The midge pupa come in a variety of sizes and colors, their body is worm like in contour. As they rise to the surface of a lake or other still water they will wiggle and occasionally stop and pause suspended. At the surface they continue to wiggle trying to break the surface tension of the water. As there heads break thru they will stop movement and start to emerge out of their pupa skins or exoskeletons (shucks) as adults.

The size and color of a midge pupa is very important to the trout which are very selective when they are feeding. The most common color is black with green, tan, brown and red following in second place. The adult midge is mosquito like in appearance with large webbed antenna off of their heads. It is surprising how large the pupa can be in relationship to the adult and experienced fly fishers use patterns up to size #8 to imitate them.

Evidence of a midge hatch is often present along the shoreline of a lake. The shucks of the pupa can be found along the waters edge usually on the down wind side of a hatch. The shucks are semi-transparent and very in color, most commonly they are cream in color. The shed skins of the pupa will help you determine the size of a midge hatch but not the color of the pupa. To find out what color the pupa is you can watch for the adult midge or try and spot an emerging pupa on the surface of the water.

The spring midge hatch is a popular annual occurrence for many fly fishers that like to start the fishing season on still water. The emergence of this early hatching insect can start as soon as the ice starts to disappear from lakes in the early spring. It is the first major insect hatch of the season and the trout key in on it very quickly.

In the Kootenay region of south eastern British Columbia there are a number of lakes that start to open up to early season angling in April every year. Due to the milder winter climate in that region, many Alberta anglers will migrate to the Kootenay's early in the spring to shake the winter blues and catch some nice sized rainbow and brook trout. The campgrounds at this time of the year are almost empty on some of the lakes and for an early season fly fisher this is a definite advantage in planning a trip.

I have fished the midge hatch on a number of occasions over the years but there are two fishing trips to BC that I remember well as some of the best fly fishing on still water that I have experienced. One of those trips was a few days spent on Summit Lake on the Crowsnest Pass area, back in the 1980's, when the trout were taking a large red midge pupa for the two days that I fished there. I landed some very big rainbow trout on that trip. The other experience that comes to mind was a few days that I spent on Premier Lake BC, also back in the 1980's.

The Premier Lake trip tops the list as a memorable outing because of the clear water in the lake and the ability to see trout in 15 feet of water as they swam over light colored marl along the bottom. I was able to sight fish for rainbows that were taking chironomids throughout the day. I first arrived at the lake in mid April and found the camp area on the south side of the lake almost empty. As is always the case when I first drive up to a lake that I plan on fishing, I drove down to the boat launch to check out the shore line and insect life.

After parking my truck, I walked down to water edge and saw that the waves had washed in thousands of midge pupa shucks onto the gravel and sand. Further up the bank in the willows the air was buzzing with clouds of midge adults and out on the lake I could see the tell tale rings of rising trout on the glassy surface of the lake, just across the bay. From that point in time it only took me a half hour to unload my canoe, find a camping spot close to the launch and start out onto the lake with all of my fishing gear.

I headed across the bay at the south end of the lake, straight to where I was seeing rising trout just off of the shore. As I paddled over the still surface, in about twenty feet of water, I could see patches of light colored marl surround by what I thought to be low growing chara weed. Marl is a light colored mixture of clay and sand like material that is common on many southern BC lakes, it makes a good back drop for spotting trout that are swimming along the bottom. It is also a good bed material for midge larva to live in at all depths.

When I got to the area where the trout were rising, I stopped paddling and let the canoe drift in toward the shore. At a depth of about 15 feet I dropped a stern anchor and one that I had rigged up for the bow of the canoe. Judging by the color of the adult midges that I had observed on the shoreline, I determined that a black color the size of the shucks at waters edge was my best bet. Before tying on a midge pupa and putting on a split shot, I threaded on a strike indicator, which is basically a float or bobber. I was using an 18 foot leader on a dry fly line which is standard for fishing lakes when a dry fly line is the choice.

After tying the fly and weight on my leader, I dropped the line into the water and when the split shot landed on the bottom of the lake bed I pulled up two feet of line and attached the strike indicator onto the leader with a tooth pick to jam it in place. By positioning the strike indicator this way, I could keep the midge pupa about one foot off of the bottom of the lake, at a depth that the trout were swimming. The only disadvantage with this type of set up is noticed when you catch a trout. When you are landing the fish you have to remove the tooth pick from the strike indicator so that it slides down the leader and you can bring in enough line to net the trout.

Casting the line out about 60 feet from the canoe I was ready for trout. The slight tilt of the indicator to an upright position signaled that the weight and fly was now at the bottom. It took only minutes before the indicator disappeared under the surface and I could see it traveling swiftly away. I had only to lift my rod tip and I felt the trout on the line. The fish immediately came to the surface and made a leap high into the air. It was a beautiful silver rainbow trout of about 18 inches.

The lake at that time was stocked with what is called a Pennask strain of rainbow trout that were first collected from Pennask Lake near Kamloops BC. This strain of Kamloops trout is known for its fighting ability and its fresh silver color. They are also a very good eating fish I might add. Soon the trout was brought to the net, admired for a brief time and then released. This sequence of events repeated itself a number of times that afternoon and evening. The largest rainbow trout that I landed and released that day was about 20 inches, but none were less than 16 inches in length.

On my second day on Premier, I discovered a good population of brook trout, many of which were very big, at a certain location on the lake. These "brookies" liked to hold close into shore, in a length of water that had a number of submerged pine trees that had fallen off of a steep bank into the water. They too took my midge patterns quite regularly and I spent the better part of a morning fishing for them.

The last day on the lake was enjoyed as much as the first and my catch of brook trout and rainbow trout continued consistently throughout the day. The black midge pattern that I had chosen the first afternoon on the water was my choice for the entire trip; I didn't need to try anything else. Fortunately I had plenty of the patterns in my fly box because I did loose a few to snags and larger trout. I finished up my last day on the water by frying up a 14 inch rainbow trout for supper before my long drive back to Alberta.

For the monofilament casting angler you can use the same set up for fishing midge imitations. With mono line and a slip bobber you will actually have an advantage in the way in which you set up your line to fish. An elastic band bobber stop can be set at any depth on the line and you can cast your fly and weight a distance with relative ease. Also, when you catch a fish you do not have to worry about removing a fixed float or strike indicator, your bobber will slide down the line to the split shot, allowing you to net your catch without difficulty. Just remember to tip your mono line with a light tippet material; it is a must when you are fishing crystal clear water like that found in Premeir Lake, BC.

Spin casting and spinning rod fishers can also use this technique with other nymph patterns such as the hare's ear nymph, the pheasant tail nymph and a variety of bead head nymphs. The nice thing about bead head nymphs is that they sink along with a split shot much faster. I have found that when I am fishing a nymph dead still in the water, if I get the nymph a little jerk every now and then, sometimes this sudden movement will entice a strike by nearby trout.

For fishing a nymph on the move you can simply attach a split shot about 3 feet up from your nymph and cast out the fly, let it sink to where you want it and then start your desired retrieve. If you're in a boat, you can troll your nymph in a steady motion or you can add a little action by jigging your rod tip. The same holds true for streamers on mono lines. With streamers you may want to get down deeper on some occasions so you may have to add extra split shot to get the job done.

When we discuss the methods of fishing still water using a fly, we have to recognize that now we are into the realm of fishing for trophy fish. Lakes throughout our province have populations of lake trout, pike and large bull trout that can reach lengths of over 30 inches and weights of over 10.lbs. It is with this in mind that I will try and cover some of the angling methods used by fly fishers to hook and land these larger species of fish. We can use the same basic techniques as we do to fish streamers in lakes to catch the larger fish, but the tackle used to accomplish this goal will be different than the standard lighter tackle used for members of the smaller trout family's.

You may cast the heavier tackle required for fishing trophy fish using the same rods and reels but the leaders and line you will need will be heavier and the fly patterns will be larger than average. However, if you are serious about fishing for larger fish on a regular basis you should be equipped with larger rods, reels and line strength. I would hate to be put in a position of trying to land a large trophy fish with small gear and tackle.

I tie patterns specifically for pike, lake trout and trophy bull trout. The hooks that I use are larger and stronger for this type of fishing. Large fish tend to feed primarily on small and medium sized bait fish, so streamers that imitate this food source are a must. The necessity of being able to get your fly down very deep in a lake will also require that you carry a good selection of heavier weights in your tackle box.

Lake trout are common throughout our province in many of the deeper and larger lakes in Alberta. During the early spring and fall of the year lake trout can be found in the shallower water areas of lakes. However, for a large portion of the fishing season they will be holding very deep in the lake, sometimes 100's of feet below the surface. In the summer months they also tend to be less active when it comes to feeding, so your presentation may have to be slowed down during the warmer months.

In the spring and late fall you can cast a streamer to lake trout from the shore or in a boat, but in the summer months you will have to troll deep from a boat to get down to where they are holding in the depths. For this slow part of the season, trolling your fly right on the bottom of the lake at a slower speed may produce some action for the angler. Northern lakes at this time of the year are always more productive because of the colder water temperatures and the short open water season.

Bull trout, although more rare in lakes, should not be over looked as a prime target for the streamer fly pattern. They are much more active than lake trout throughout the summer months and will readily take a streamer fished along the shoreline or in the deeper water. In my area, the lower Kananaskis Lake has a great bull trout fishery, and recently the upper Kananaskis has been stocked with bull trout as well.

I have done quite well fishing the lower Kananaskis in June and July during the summer. Fishing from a float tube out from shore, I like to cast my streamer into the shore line and then let it drop down the drop off a bit before I start my retrieve. Bull trout are not shy about large streamer patterns and I found that when I first started fishing for bull trout I would use pike streamers that were tied on 2/0 streamer hooks. Since then I have started tying streamer patterns specifically for bull trout and I prefer to use a size 2,4 and 6 long shank hook for the majority of the flies that I tie for this purpose.

Pike are a great sport fish in our province and it wasn't until recently that fly fishing for them has grown into a major sport fishing opportunity for many fly fishers. With the technology that has been developed to cast to these larger trophy fish, you can easily acquire all that you will need in most sporting goods stores or fly shops. The new thin diameter steel leaders that you'll need are far better than those that fly fishers first were faced with using not too many years earlier.

I have fished for pike with a fly on both a sinking and floating line. My preferred streamer pattern is a large buck tail streamer tied inverted so that it is weed-less in design. Inverted means that the pattern is tied with the buck tail on the bottom side of a hook and it is weighted so that it will swim upside down thru the water. The buck tail hairs cover the bend of the hook and allow it to travel thru weeds without snagging up or collecting them in the bend of the hook.

Pike love to hang out in the weeds, in the cover of weeds they can wait in ambush to capture their prey, the weed-less designed streamer patterns are great for fishing in weedy habitat. Other streamer patterns that are used for pike have weed guards built into their design, for the same purpose. Swimming a weed-less streamer thru a weed bank or along its edge is always a good method for hooking large pike.

When I first started tying buck-tail streamers for pike I had no idea that they would be effect on walleye. I had given a few patterns to a fishing buddy of mine for fishing pike on the prairie lakes in Alberta and Saskatchewan. I was pleased to learn later on that he had used the patterns on walleye and had done well. I have yet to try fishing for walleye with a fly rod but I look forward to the opportunity.

Above Photo: Angler Barry Baldwin with a couple of Ghost Lake Trout.

Reservoirs

Unlike lakes, reservoirs have water levels that fluctuate throughout the year; this is especially evident on power generating reservoirs and to a lesser extent on irrigation reservoirs. This instability in the water levels along the shoreline, limits the food production that fish require to maintain healthy numbers, in comparison with a stable lake environment. However, this does not rule out good angling for trout, whitefish, pike and walleye on these man-made still water habitats.

In our area we have a number of power generation reservoirs that still provide a recreational opportunity for anglers. The Kananaskis Lakes and the Spray Lakes are good examples in point. Despite an unstable shoreline environment, both of these water bodies are destinations for anglers throughout the season. This does not mean that they wouldn't be far better fisheries if the water levels were more stable but under the circumstances they are included as viable fisheries.

The same holds true for many prairie irrigation reservoirs that have pike and walleye populations or they are stocked with rainbow trout. Most of the techniques used for fishing lakes apply to reservoirs. Points, bays, weed beds and shallow humps are all good locations to find fish. The actual dam itself, if re-enforced with rock rip-rap can be a good piece of structure to fish. Small bait fish and other insect life inhabit the rocky habitat of rip-rap and this draws in the sport fish that feed on both.

Stocked Ponds and Prairie Potholes

For beginning anglers, especially children, the stocked trout pond is a great destination for your first attempt at catching a fish. Some stocked trout ponds are close to home and are open to the public; others can be accessed by permission or by a pay to fish basis. The idea of paying to fish may be repulsive to some but for a young child that is not a priority. Fishing a well managed pond will allow young potential anglers an opportunity to catch their first fish and establish whether the sport is in their interests or not.

If you have a desire to fish larger still water you can find a prairie pot-hole lake that is stocked by the province annually for recreation. You can refer to the Alberta Fish and Wildlife Division's provincial regulations to find out a list of stocked lakes in the province. Sporting goods stores are also a great source for information when it comes to destinations to fish. It is in their best interest to keep your interest in the sport by sending you to a good location. They are always up to date on the latest reports on most area water bodies that are stocked for angling.

An angler can use the same lake angling techniques on trout ponds and prairie pothole lakes. Fishing a streamer or nymph on the move with a

68

weight of split shot or still fishing a nymph under a slip bobber are both a good approach to catching the stocked trout that you are after. If you plan on keeping a trout or two for the pan you should be prepared to preserve the flesh of the fish in a good manor. The first step in keeping your catch in good form is to clean it on site.

If you have a cooler with ice you can lay the fish on top of the ice wrapped in damp newspaper and a plastic bag. Ice is great for keeping your catch cool but if you don't have any, just the damp newspaper will suffice. Always keep the fish out of direct sun light or warm air. When you get home you can rinse the fish off and prepare it for cooking or refrigerate or freeze it. If you decide to freeze the fish make sure that it is wrapped in a plastic container that has had the air removed as best as possible. I would not keep the fish frozen for longer than 1 month before consumption.

River Safety

Before we close this particular chapter on fishing water let us take a brief look at some important safety issues. Most safety concerns can be addressed by the simply using common sense; however, there are some hidden dangers that anglers may not be aware of involving some of the flowing waters mentioned in this book. In the immediate area there are a few flowing waters that are subject to sudden fluctuations in water levels from power generation plants located along their course.

The Kananaskis River and the middle and upper Bow River have dams on their systems that cause the water levels in their channels to suddenly rise without warning. It would be helpful to know the exact times of this occurrence, however, it is all subject to which stream system you're fishing on, to know when the water will rise at a given time. The best practice is to be aware of this daily program and be careful when you wade and where you wade to.

You can check the water line along the shore when you arrive at the stream or river to determine whether the water levels at the time are low or high, or you can check with an area resident that is familiar with the daily fluctuations. What ever the case, just be careful out there. There have been incidents that have happened to me and other anglers over the years on the Bow River that have led to an awareness that is ever present and a knowledge of this river system that should be share with all new comers.

Around the Town of Cochrane anglers have lost tackle boxes and gone for unplanned swims in their waders over the years. After fishing the Bow River in this area for a number of years you become familiar with some of the warning signs that the river is coming up in level. The most common warning signs are the sound of a surge of water coming downstream toward you, it is some what subtle to notice but you develop an ear for it. The other, is the advance of water onto the dry shoreline rocks which usually confirms the first warning sign.

On the upper Bow River it is different though, there are areas where the river breaks up into channels and if you access the river during low flow time periods, you can unknowingly wade across channels to access different areas of the river. When the water comes up on the upper Bow, it is less noticeable than in the Cochrane area, and sound and the wetting of shoreline rocks are not as easily noticed. The banks are covered with grass and treed with timber on this reach of the river, so identifying the existing water levels requires a little more attention.

I have been nearly stranded on islands on the upper Bow River in the past when the water levels came up suddenly, but the most memorable and scary experience that I have had was during the early spring season on the upper Bow. I had waded into a run on the river to fish for early brown trout and eastern brook trout one morning. The night before was a cold one and ice had formed in some of the back waters and slow moving channels in the river.

In the later part of the morning the water levels started coming up with out me being aware, as I was concentrating on my fly fishing. A large sheet of ice that was about 1/2 inch thick had broken away from an area upstream and had floated down to me with the rising water. When it hit the back of my legs the force nearly knocked me over but I managed to turn around as it pushed me downstream and start breaking thru it with my knees and feet. The event happened so fast that I didn't have time to realize my situation. Somehow I managed to break my way thru the ice to the shoreline.

Because of the size of the sheet of ice there was no way I could have stopped or slowed its drift in the river. I was fortunate enough to be able to break thru its thickness by using my legs and feet while wearing neoprene chest waders. I was also very lucky not to be standing that deep in the water. After making it safely to shore the reality of the experience had time to sink in and I feel today as much as back then that I was very lucky that I didn't go for a swim in the frigid waters. I was fishing by myself that day. It is experiences like this one that has made me develop a tremendous respect for the safety issues that one must follow when fishing big water.

Part Six

The Sport Fish of Alberta

The east slopes of the Rocky Mountains and the prairies to the east provide a multitude of angling opportunities for a number of different sport fish. If you are a trout fisher there are brook trout, bull trout, rainbow trout, Brown trout, cutthroat trout and lake trout to choose from. Other sport fish that are sought after are mountain whitefish, Lake Whitefish, grayling, pike, walleye and perch. This province supports a wide variety of fish to angle for year round.

The variety of trout species that are available today can be attributed to the stocking of non-native trout from eastern Canada, the US and parts of Europe. The only native trout present when the settlers first moved to Alberta were the bull trout, cutthroat trout, lake trout and a tiny population of Athabasca River rainbow trout. When the railroad first made it to the Rocky Mountains to the west of the City of Calgary, eastern brook trout were transported from down east and stock in many lakes and streams in the Banff area.

In 1913 a fish hatchery was built and started operation in the Town of Banff. Trout from all over were purchased for the hatchery and used to stock the waters of rivers, lakes and streams of the eastern slopes area. In the 1920's Brown trout from Scotland were accidentally stocked into a tributary of the Bow River near the Town of Canmore. Later on Brown trout from Germany made their way into the Banff Hatchery and became the preferred strain for stocking area streams.

In the 1930's rainbow trout that were purchased from Montana, Idaho, Vancouver Island and Cranbrook BC, were planted in many tributaries of the Bow River and area lakes. The middle and lower Bow River at the time supported a population of native cutthroat trout and Bull trout. In the 30's some of the tributaries of the Bow River such as Three Point Creek and Highwood River were stocked with rainbow trout.

During the same decade both a Scottish Loch Leven strain and later a German strain of brown trout were introduced into the some of the head water tributaries of the Red Deer River system. Streams such as the Dogpound, Little Red, Fallentimber and the Raven were suitable habitats for the European brown trout.

Today it would be very hard to determine which species are from which source supplier because of the hybridization of the many different strains. The modern method of DNA analyses has opened new doors of opportunity to trace back some of the existing populations that are present in our area today. As I write this book there are already programs under-way to start this process.

Fortunately there are still a few native strains of east slopes trout that are thriving in modern times, thanks in part to some knowledgeable provincial fisheries managers that took measures to protect them. The Job Lake cutthroat trout, the Smith Dorrian Creek bull trout and the Minne-wanka lake trout for example. These two cutthroat and bull trout native strains are protected and their pure genetics is being used to restock a variety of water bodies.

The Job Lake cutthroat trout is an original Spray Lakes strain of east slopes cutthroat trout probably related to the original Bow River and Kananaskis River strain. In 1917 the Banff trout hatchery opened up a sub-hatchery on the Lower Spray Lake, where a creek from the Upper Lake entered the Lower Lake there was a forest warden's cabin and the new hatchery was built next to it. In the spring of the year, cutthroat trout eggs were collected from trout that congregated at the inflowing creek. The eggs were incubated, hatched and then used to stock area lakes and streams.

The Lower Kananaskis Lake was reported to provide the best cut-throat trout fishery in the mountains around the turn of the century. The Morley Stoney Indians frequented the lower lake to catch cutthroat trout for food, annually. However, this strain is considered extinct in modern times. There are some wild cutthroat trout present in some of the headwa-ters of tributaries to the Kananaskis River today, but by having no DNA from the original strain of the Lower Lake, it is unlikely that a connection between them can be proven.

The Lower Kananaskis Lake is well known for the trophy bull trout that are present in its waters today. Alberta record bull trout have earned this water body a reputation for being the destination in the province for large bull trout. This resource was in danger of disappearing in the last decade but thanks to fisheries managers and a number of dedicated clubs and individuals the famous bull of the Smith Dorrien is doing well under its new protective management policy. These large fish can still be angled for in modern times but there is a strict catch and release guideline that anglers must comply with.

In recent years the strain of the Lower Lake bull trout has been introduced into the Upper Kananaskis Lake along with a native Job Lake strain of cutthroat trout. Hopefully this introduction will be successful one for both species, but it will take some time to access the success of the restocking. Because there are no known reproductive opportunities for both the bull and cutthroat trout on the Upper Lake, the program will be an ongoing stocking program, unless a tributary to the upper lake is adopted by the fish as an environment to reproduce.

The Minnewanka lake trout is a majestic species of long living and slow growing trout that reaches huge proportions in the deep waters of the lake. Annually, lake trout of 30 to 40 plus pounds are caught in the lake, usually around the opening day of the season when the trout are found in the shallower waters of the lake. For trophy anglers this trout is the ultimate catch for fresh water lakes. There are lake trout in other area lakes such as the Spray Lakes reservoir, Ghost dam reservoir and Bearspaw dam reservoir but the Minnewanka giants are the target for serious lake trout fisherman west of Calgary.

Rainbow Trout

Now that we have reviewed a brief history of the trout fishery in the south central east slopes let us take a close look at each individual species, their habits, habitats and their status in an anglers list of preference. To start with we have to turn our attention to the rainbow trout. This species is the most sought after of the trout family in all of North America. It also holds a very high standing in many different parts of the world.

As previously mentioned, there is a native strain of rainbow trout that is and was present on the Athabasca River system from the Jasper Park area downstream to an area near the Town of Hinton. From any reports that I have read about this strain of trout it was relatively small in size compared to other strains on the west slopes of the Rocky Mountains.

The waters that flow into the Pacific Ocean are the true home waters of the rainbow trout. Over time, certain strains of the rainbow trout were land locked into lake systems in the province of British Columbia. Two of the most popular lake strains known to fresh water anglers in BC are the Kamloops strain and the Kootney strain of rainbow trout. Both species are known to grow to very large size and therefore they have been used to stock many of the lakes throughout BC.

The Kamloops, Kootenay strain of fresh water rainbow trout have been known to reach weights of over 20.lbs in some lakes in the province. However, the vast majority are common up to around 10.lbs in weight. The all time record Kootenay trout was killed with a gaff by George White on Jewel Lake BC in 1913 and it weighed 56.lbs. It may be interesting for you to know that George killed another trout that was with this monster on the same evening and it weighed in at 48.lbs. Since that evening there have been other monster rainbows caught out of the lake by angling, one more at 48.lbs by two unknown American anglers in the 1930's.

From the time that the first two giants were gaffed in Jewel Lake until a period in the 1940's a number of Jewel Lake giants were caught and killed. It has been said that poison from the mining operations on the lake eventually killed off the last of this magnificent strain of rainbow trout, there has not been any trout of such huge proportion caught in the lake since the 1930's. What a shame to loose such an interesting strain of giant trout.

The other common strain of rainbow trout located on the west slopes of the Rockies is the steelhead trout. This spectacular species returns from the Ocean to reproduce in the west slopes fresh water streams annually. It is during this spawning migration that anglers ply the waters hoping to hook a steelhead trout. When the steelhead migrates down to the Ocean, after a short period of time spent in fresh water streams as a juvenile, it experiences tremendous growth rates by feeding on a rich diet of Ocean forage, before it returns to the fresh water to spawn as an adult.

Steelhead trout are reputed to be very hard to catch on a fly but recent developments in modern fishing methods have improved the odds and reduced the challenge, making it a popular sport fishing pastime with many an angler. With what once took many hours to achieve, today's angler can accomplish in a much shorter time, the hooking of a steelhead migrating up a freshwater river or stream is one of the ultimate goals of many a fly fisher.

Our east slopes variety of rainbow trout are much smaller than the lake and sea run variety just mentioned, however, some of them do exhibit similar traits to the steelhead trout during the early spring spawning migration. The famous Bow River strain of rainbow trout are well known for their long journeys during the spawning season, and the coloration on many of them is quite similar to that of the coastal steelhead trout. I find this is especially true of the Jumpingpound Creek strain of the middle Bow River.

The large Jumpingpound trout that occupy a habitat in the Bearspaw reservoir for most of the fishing season; move up into the JP Creek in the spring of the year to spawn. In general, they are steel grey in color and are know to travel up to 35 km from the reservoir to spawn in the JP Creek. I have fished this run of trout for many years and I can see the resemblance that they have in comparison to some of the steelhead that I have caught on Vancouver Island.

When the Banff trout hatchery was first buying trout for its stocking programs in the 1930's, it purchased rainbow trout from Montana and Idaho. The Idaho hatchery was located on the Snake River where there were runs of steelhead still present in the Snake River. I also have read that Banff had purchased fish from a trout hatchery on the Cowichan River on Vancouver Island where there were also steelhead trout. I have heard many a comment from experienced Bow River fisherman that feel the same way, about the strain of rainbow that are present on the Lower Bow River and move up the Highwood River system to spawn.

The rainbow trout populations that are fished for the most, in the south central area of Alberta, are present in the Bow River watershed and south down to the Oldman River and Crowsnest River region of the province. There are a few stream populations here and there in the northern areas of Alberta but presently they do not receive as much attention, except for the lake populations that are stocked on an annual basis.

The rainbow trout is a spring spawning trout and on flowing streams and rivers where there is a wild population, the main stem or tributaries where they spawn are closed during the spring of the season. Before and after this reproductive phase, the rainbow trout provides a lot of recreation for the trout angler. They are veracious insect feeders and will take a fly quite readily. Rainbow trout are known to be an easy trout to catch in most environments, when compared to other trout such as brown trout. The average life span of the rainbow trout is 6 to 7 years of age.

The rainbow trout that are stocked annually in prairie pothole lakes and reservoirs can grow very fast with an ample food supply. If these trout winter over for a few years and they are not killed by anglers, they can grow to a very large size. Winter kill occurs when the available oxygen levels drop below the minimum required to sustaining trout. This lack of oxygen can result from an over abundance of aquatic weed growth that uses oxygen when it decays during the winter months.

If a lake has proper depth and there is enough late fall wave action to saturate the lake with oxygen, prior to ice formation, trout will usually be able to winter over and the by product can be a good population of larger rainbow trout. From year to year word travels around about good size rainbow trout that are being caught on different lakes throughout the province. Once anglers find out about the big trout on a certain water body, they are fished heavily until their numbers decline. However, the program of restocking trout continues, as a new batch of trout grows into maturity, the rumors of large trout starts all over again.

I can recall a time back in the late 1980's when reports of giant rainbow trout were being caught on Crawling Valley reservoir. It was a fairly new reservoir built by the Eastern Irrigation District on a canal from the Bow River. When the lake was first flooded it was stocked initially with rainbow trout. Due to the rich food supply available, in particular fresh water shrimp, the trout grew at an enormous rate and for a few years reports of trout of 15 to 20 pounds in weight were heard in at all of the city of Calgary sporting goods stores.

Crawling Valley was suddenly the top angling destination for die hard lake fishers that liked to catch big rainbow trout. However, this trophy rainbow trout fishery was destine to disappear in the near future. The reservoir was soon stocked with walleye, pike, Lake Whitefish and perch that replaced the rainbow trout stocking program. For a few years, the rainbow trout ruled but the provincial government was looking for a sport fish population that could reproduce annually without stocking. There are still a few rainbow trout that make their way down the irrigation canal from the Bow River into Crawling Valley, but reports of their capture in the lake are few and far in between. The present day Alberta record for a rainbow trout caught by angling is 20.lbs 4 oz.

Brown Trout

Next on my list of sport fish is the wary brown trout. This European species of trout has been fished for centuries by anglers in Britain and Europe. This could be why the trout is reputed to be so much more difficult to catch than some of the North American trout species. Years of having a fly or bait presented to them by knowledgeable fishers may have cropped out the less wary trout; it may have something to do with Darwin's theory of "The process of natural selection". In any case, the brown trout is regarded by most anglers as the ultimate prize for a trout fisher.

In the earlier 1900's both the Scottish strain and the German strain of brown trout were stocked into our area waters, but the German brown turned out to be the most popular with fisheries managers. However, there are still Loch Leven brown trout genes in the Bow River brown trout populations. The difference in appearance between the two trout is the coloration. The German Brown has the common red and black spots so typical to most brown trout that we catch today. The Loch Leven has large black spots but does not display the orange spots of the German variety.

Brown trout are fall spawning trout; they start their spawning activity in October and continue as late as December. During this period of time many brown trout waters are closed for angling. The season is usually closed for angling after October 31st every fall. A brown trout's life span can average between 8 to 9 years for most trout. During the angling season brown trout are a challenge to catch. They are known to be some what particular about what they feed on and some days it is a real puzzle to figure out what fly pattern to use. The brown is also more adapted to feed early in the day and later in the afternoon and evening, with some anglers fishing them after dark on some waters.

On the lower Bow River I find that the brown trout are easier to catch than on many other waters that I fish. This could be related to the fact that the trout populations are so much higher on the Bow, and trout are aggressively competitive for any available food item. On some of the smaller waters and lakes that I fish for brown trout, they can be very difficult on some days, but over time I find that my knowledge of how to fish for them is growing. It is of major importance that you present your fly delicately and approach a potential trout holding spot with stealth.

Brown trout are very territorial in nature, and prefer to find their own little niche of habitat where the competition is minimal. This will often result in finding brown trout holding in what many would consider unlikely holding water. Shallow undercuts on stream banks, a little over head cover in shallower water or a small piece of pocket water that many anglers might past by. I think that some of these attributes may help make the brown trout such an interesting sport fish to angle for.

Brown trout have very hard boney mouths that are sometimes difficult to penetrate with even a sharp hook. I like to use hooks of a smaller size with the barb bent down to improve my catch rates. If I see a small ring on the water that could be a rising brown trout I will try and imitate the small insects that the trout is eating. I have hooked brown trout of over 22 inches on size 20 and smaller hooks, and landed them. This feeding habit of brown trout is sometimes related to their finicky nature, they are opportunist for some food items, even if they are the smallest insects on the water but you have to match the hatch in both size and color. However, when there is no insect activity related to hatches, the larger fish usually prefer a big meal.

Once a brown trout has reached near maturity, they tend to have a preference for a diet of small fish. Their hunt for minnows and small fish makes them a good target for the streamer fly fisher and most Bow River guides know this and take advantage of the fishing method quite regularly. The larger male trout are equipped with a mouth designed for larger prey, and their teeth sometimes will require a heavier line or leader to avoid breaking them off.

The brown trout has sensitive eye sight that makes them shy from bright sunny days, this desire to keep in the shade or out of direct sun light, compels the brown trout to seek any available over head cover for shelter and a place to hold. Their attraction to any habitat that can hide their presence or keep them in low light makes them a target for the trained eye of the experienced angler. When I fish for browns on streams that have a tangle of submerged wood or rocky cover I am constantly on the look out for any likely brown trout holds that provide shade and overhead cover. On lakes, any submerged debris or weed bed can give up a few brown trout if you can keep your fly from snagging up.

One of my favorite brown trout lake's, is Gap Lake, near the Town of Exshaw, Alberta. It is a relatively shallow lake that is spring fed and has an out flow that enters the Bow River. The lake has very clear water and on a calm day you can see the brown trout swimming along the bottom over a lake bed made up of marl and chara weed. This area is known for its winds and finding a calm day is rare.

During the early mornings you can usually beat the breeze and get a few hours of sight fishing in before the wind and the waves come up. Late in the evening is also a good time to fish Gap. When there is a hatch, the trout will feed on the submerged nymphs and the surface dry flies, as it takes place you can see the brown trout on the move looking for a meal. Other days they will just swim along the bottom, looking for shrimp or larva.

In 1989 the Sarcee Fish and Game Association installed a number of submerged reefs made of woody debris in the lake. I will often position my boat or float tube close by one or more of these man made reefs to fish. I prefer a boat for this type of angling because you can stand and get a better view of the trout moving about on the bottom. When the trout are feeding, I have found that they seem to travel in a pattern and once you have established this feeding lane you can cast to the trout or to the general area that they move in.

This type of sight fishing is the best experience that a lake angler can have and I have left Gap Lake with memories of some great fishing on a number of occasions. The lake has a reputation of giving up some very large brown trout in the 7 to 8.lb range. My personal best was a large buck brown trout that measured 26 inches and weighed 7 ½ .lbs, I caught the trout back in the 1980's and I still remember the detailed memories of the catch. The present day Alberta record brown trout weighed in at 17.lbs 9 oz. and it was caught on Swan Lake near the Town of Caroline.

Brook Trout

Brook trout are one of the more beautiful members of the trout family and they are loved by many a small creek angler. They are very prolific in nature and are found in great abundance in many small creeks throughout the eastern slopes area. Brook trout are also known to inhabit areas of streams where other species would not.

I was riding a horse with a friend in the foothills of the Rockies on a fall morning one time when I stopped to let my horse drink from a small pool in a drainage channel at the bottom of the draw. When the horse dipped its head to drink, a small brook trout darted out from under a rock and alarmed the horse. The small brook trout must have migrated up the channel during the spring rains and ended up stranded in the small pool.

Brook trout reach maturity at a very early age, between 2 and 4 years. They can spawn in conditions much less favorable to other trout species, which makes them true survivors in many environments. Most stream trout require a rocky or gravel bottom to make their egg nests (redds) in but brook trout are the exception. I have witnessed brook trout spawning in a spring upwelling and below a beaver dam in a tangle of silt and willow.

Small creek brook trout normally don't grow to any great size living in smaller creeks but I have fished some waters where they would grow up to 16 inches in length when the fishing pressure is low and they are usually quite full bodied when they are mature adults. The Alberta record catch for brook trout was 15.lbs and the trout was caught in Pine lake, in Wood Buffalo National Park, Alberta in 1967. Their smaller size doesn't seem to matter when you are fishing for them. What brook trout lack in length they make up in sporting quality.

Brook trout are always eager to take a fly and will give you a good battle when hooked. They are fall spawning trout that start to spawn in late September and early October and they are usually finished spawning by late October. Prior to the fall spawning period they become a beautiful mix of color with the males being the more intense in orange, red and dark olive, with bright white strips along their bottom fins. On many brook trout waters the season closes for angling around October 1 every fall. The average maximum life span of brook trout in Alberta is 5 years.

Cutthroat Trout

The cutthroat trout is Alberta's true original trout species for the east slopes, apart from the Athabasca rainbow trout which was exclusive to the Athabasca River system; the cutthroat trout was present on most east slopes streams in central and southern parts of the province. The lake trout and bull trout are actually members of the char family, so this excludes them from being a true trout species. Cutthroat trout are quite similar to rainbow trout in appearance except for the red/orange slits that are present on the underside of the cutthroat trout's gill plates.

Rainbow trout and cutthroat trout spawn at around the same time in the spring of the year and cutthroat are known to hybridize with rainbow trout. These hybrids are known as cut-bow's and as a fisher you will here this term used regularly in fishing conversations. However, the term cut/bow is over used and it can be attributed to color variation between cutthroat trout on many streams, lakes and rivers.

Above Photo: A Waiparous Creek cutthroat trout.

A good case in point is the Waiparous Creek variety, northwest of Calgary. The Waiparous Creek variety of cutthroat are often referred to as cut-bow's but the creek hasn't been stocked with rainbows since the 1950's. DNA sampling done of a population of cutthroat trout present in a tributary of the Waiparous Creek showed that they are true pure strain cutthroat trout. The cutthroat trout found in the main creek channel are very light in color with smaller red/orange slits under their gills; this could be what leads to the confusion.

The cutthroat trout lives a rather short life span of about 5 to 6 years on many waters, but in that growth period they can reach a size of about 20 inches. However, the normal maximum size range for small stream cutthroat trout is around 14 inches. Lake raised cutthroat trout can reach a very large size in comparison to stream cutthroat. Many high mountain lakes provide good recreation for those that don't mind a bit of a hike to fish for them. The Alberta record for a cutthroat trout caught by angling is 9.lbs 9 ounces.

The cutthroat trout are a very good sport fish and are always eager to take a fly. You can find cutthroat trout on many of the same type's of small creeks that eastern brook trout inhabit. The introduction of the brook trout has resulted in the disappearance of many a native strain of the cutthroat trout in the province. The brook trout are known to over take cutthroat trout waters when introduced or by natural migration. The introduction of brook trout in the southern part of the province was less prevalent in the early part of the century and as a result some of the best cutthroat trout waters are further to the south.

Before the introduction of rainbow trout and brown trout into our major rivers like the Bow River, the cutthroat trout was quite common. Today you can still catch the occasional cutthroat trout in the Bow River, especially between the Ghost Dam and the Bearspaw Dam. The cutthroat trout that are found in this reach are most likely wash downs from the Ghost Reservoir or Jumpingpound Creek. The Waiparous Creek enters the Ghost River which flows into the Ghost Lake from the northwest; as a result there is a very small resident population of cutthroat trout in the Ghost Lake.

In recent years there have been measures taken by fisheries managers to help protect some of the remaining cutthroat trout populations in the central east slopes region. A zero catch limit on all cutthroat trout has resulted in signs of a slow recovery for this threatened species of native trout on many waters. Identifying the remaining known populations of resident stream cutthroat by the use of DNA will help us better understand the origin of many isolated populations of this trout.

In the first months of January of 2008, the Department of Fisheries and Oceans Canada declared the cutthroat trout in the province of Alberta a "species at risk" which is close to the former classification of "threatened species", I think!

Bull Trout

The bull trout is another native Alberta trout that is receiving some special attention these days. There was a time back in the early to mid 1900's when the bull trout was viewed as a veracious pest that was eating all of the preferred trout populations in many of Alberta's streams and rivers. They were also very easy prey for the bait fishers that were out to get them. A decline in numbers over the years led to a recovery program that got underway in the 1990's. Fortunately, there was still a reasonable population left to protect and in the latter part of the 90's and into the new century we can already see some positive results.

Bull trout are similar in appearance to the eastern brook trout; this has led to a national advertising campaign to educate the angling public about the differences in features between the two fish. The most popular identification characteristic is the lack of black spots on the dorsal fin on the back of the bull trout compared to the black spotting on the dorsal fin of the brook trout. The bull trout has pink, yellow, orange or pinkish red colored spots on its side compared to red spots with a blue halo on brook trout. The tail fin on the bull trout is also more forked than the square like tail on a brook trout. Bull trout usually have a wide and some what flat head compared to eastern brook trout.

The bull trout can grow to a much greater size than the brook trout, due to its relatively long life span and a consistent diet of other fish. Some female bull trout will not reach sexual maturity until they are 8 to 9 years of age. Bull trout spawn in the late summer and early fall of the year with some spawning occurring in August and continuing into September.

A number of streams in the province are presently still open to angling when the bull trout are spawning, so caution should be exercised when you wade in streams where bull trout are present. Like other trout, a nest or redd is excavated into the gravel bottom of a stream for the laying of eggs by a female bull trout. The redds can be hard to distinguish on some streams because of the cleaner gravel found on many mountain streams, so try and avoid these gravel areas when wading or crossing a stream.

I have heard stories of huge brook trout being caught in the head waters of small streams over the years. I suspect that these large trout are most likely mature bull trout. When the bull trout is in its spawning colors it is a beautiful specimen with bright orange or red bellies on the males and a prominent white leading edge on its lower fins, much the same as male brook trout in spawning colors. These large bulls that are caught in headwaters in the late summer are most likely there to spawn.

Juvenile bull trout start out their life feeding on insects just like any other trout's diet, but when they reach a large enough size they will switch to a total fish diet which makes them a major predator on many streams. As is the case with most large trout that feed on other fish, they will not feed that often, when they do, they usually make it worth their while and will take a good sized fish for a meal.

I continue to hear stories of large bull trout coming into shore, chasing some angler's cutthroat trout or whitefish that they have hooked. In some cases the large bulls are successful and grab the smaller fish before the angler can catch it, or they will simply wait until the angler releases the fish before attacking it. Released fish are usually in a state of shock when they are let go back into the water and in this state will be unable to escape the waiting jaws of a large bull; I really think that some bull trout know this and take advantage of the circumstances when ever possible.

During the juvenile years of a bull trout's life they can provide a fly fisher with some great recreation. I have had a number of tremendous day's on the water, dry fly fishing for smaller bull trout on streams like the Burnt Timber River. Later on when the bull reaches the fish feeding years the streamer fly is the best bet and the size of fly that you use can be very large in length. When I first started fishing the Lower Kananaskis Lake I used a pike streamer to catch bull trout, and the pattern worked very well I might add.

The present catch and release record for a bull trout caught in the province of Alberta was a 17.lb 11.7 oz. bull trout. There is a good chance that now that these tremendous trout are protected, in years to come we will see trout of new record size being caught and released. With the stocking of the Upper Kananaskis Lake a few years ago and a good population of suckers in the lake for these fish to feed on, we can expect another trophy fishery to slowly take shape.

The lake trout or gray trout as some anglers call it, is the king of the trout water. These trout are known to grow to enormous size inspiring many a local legend. The world's largest lake trout was taken from Lake Athabasca in 1961 and weighed in at 102.lbs. Lake trout are gray or grayish green in color and have vermiculations on their back similar to those found on brook trout. On their sides there are lighter gray or olive grey spots which can be hard to distinguish on some of the brighter colored varieties.

When lake trout are young they will feed on various aquatic lake insects but when they are old enough to prey on small fish their diet changes. Lake trout are deep water fish and prefer lakes that have deep cool water. In the spring and fall of the year you can find lake trout in shallower water feeding but when the water temperature starts to raise the trout retreat to the safety of the depths. They spawn in shallow or moderate depths over a rubble or boulder strewn bed on well aerated areas of a lake.

Unlike the rest of the trout family they do not dig a nest or redd in gravel but rather broadcast their eggs over larger sized lake bed material. Their spawning season usually starts earlier around September up in the northern climates, but in central Alberta it runs from about October thru to November. The lake trout lives a very long life compared to other trout species. In the cold northern waters they can live over 50 years but in the south where the water temperatures are warmer they will live around 15 to 20 years of age. The Alberta angling record for lake trout was a 52.lb 8 oz. trout.

The south central region of Alberta has a very small lake trout fishery in comparison to the northern part of the province. In the Calgary area there are three reservoirs that hold a population of lake trout and one popular Banff National Park lake that is a common destination for those after a trophy lake trout. The Spray Lakes, Ghost Lake and Bearspaw reservoirs all have lake trout in their waters. The Spray Lake and Ghost Lake are the most popular fishing locations outside of the park.

In Banff National Park Lake Minnewanka is the best known lake for trophy lake trout. Its deep waters give up huge fish annually to anglers that know how to fish the lake and occasionally a beginner hooks a big one. The Spray Lakes is actually one lake that was flooded over two lakes when the reservoir was built. It has a good population of smaller lake trout but it has also been known to produce the odd "lunker" every season.

In 1984 I was one those fortunate enough to catch one of these larger lake trout in the Ghost reservoir. I was fishing off of the shoreline in the early spring of the year over a deep drop off in the old river channel on the lake. I had just arrived and cast my offering out into the lake about 30 meters from shore when the big lake trout hit my hook as it was sinking. I set the hook but missed the fish so I continued to let it sink toward bottom. As my line hit the bottom the trout hit for a second time and I set the hook into it. Immediately the giant trout make a long run out into the lake, for a minute I wondered if I had enough line on my reel to accommodate the fish but at about 170 meters the trout stopped its run and over a period of 20 minutes I was able to land the big lake trout.

The lake trout was 39 inches long and weighed 28.lbs. It was a true trophy fish for the Ghost Lake and I decided to get it mounted for my own bragging rights. Since that time there have been plenty larger fish caught out of the Ghost but in my mind the trophy that I caught that day was the biggest and the best, especially considering the amount of time that I had spent trying for a large Ghost Lake trout. If I caught a trout of equal or larger size today, I would release it alive. Since that first trophy experience I have learned how long a lake trout has to live to achieve such a size and I would feel guilty if I once again killed such a fish. I always pack a camera for such an occasion, and if I catch another - a picture will suffice.

The Ghost reservoir is a tough fishery for anglers trying to catch lake trout. However, it too has a few very large lake trout that are caught every season. The Ghost and Spray are great locations for winter ice fishing and this is when they produce their highest numbers of lake trout for the anglers that don't mind the sudden weather changes typical to both waters.

The lakes trout is very tolerant of cold water and more active than other cold water species when the temperatures get close to 0 degrees on some reservoirs during the winter months.

Rocky Mountain Whitefish

The Rocky Mountain whitefish is the most common sport fish found on our area's rivers and lakes. They are well adapted at competing with all of the different trout species and tend to feed on the variety of smaller insect life that is abundant in most waters. As a result of their preference for small food items, nature's evolutionary process has developed them with a very small mouth. For this reason anglers that are targeting mountain whitefish use smaller flies to catch them.

Mountain whitefish are fall spawner's; they start their migration up rivers and streams in mid September and start to spawn in early October. Prior to spawning whitefish are the focus of many angers for their shear numbers in rivers and streams during the fall migration. During the fall run it is not uncommon for anglers to catch large numbers of this fish. They are relatively small in size but have a life span of about 8 to 9 years of age. The current Alberta record for a mountain whitefish is a 5.lb 10.5 oz. fish.

Unlike the trout family they have large scales and are mono toned in color. During the fall period prior to spawning and when the migration is underway the whitefish has provided a great fishing opportunity for many anglers over the years. I can recall years ago on the Bow River in Cochrane, anglers would congregate at what we called "Griffin's Bend" to catch the fall run whitefish. Every weekend throughout the month of September car loads of anglers would be pulling into the field near the big fishing hole, rods tackle boxes and lawn chairs in tow. At the end of the morning fish when the water in the river had risen, scores of anglers would make their way back to their cars with stringers of whitefish dangling in the morning light. It seemed like people had more time for recreation back in those days.

The whitefish is a common catch among fly fishers, they will take a fly readily, especially a nymph. I have even caught whitefish on streamer patterns. The most popular method of catching "rockies" for spin fishing enthusiasts is with a baited fly, maggots being preferred. There is a trick to baiting a fly with a maggot. You have to hook them thru the head area.

The big problem is that most anglers think that the head is the pointed area of the body. That is actually the tail, maggots travel backwards and the head is the flat end of the larva. It is at this spot on a maggot that you hook onto your fly. Just under the skin, this keeps the maggot alive and wiggling.

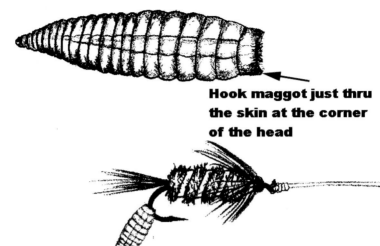

**Hook maggot just thru
the skin at the corner
of the head**

The mountain whitefish are good fighting fish that will entertain any angler when hooked, especially during the late season migration run. They prefer pools, runs, eddy's and riffles to hold in and are known to maintain a position in faster water than trout during the fall season. During the fall season larger fish in the 16 to 18 inch size range can be caught more readily on the Bow River. Many of these larger whitefish move up from the big pools and the reservoirs to actively feed in the river system.

Lake Whitefish

The lake whitefish is a close relative of the mountain whitefish and it inhabits lakes and reservoirs throughout the province. On average the lake whitefish grows to a much larger size than its cousin the mountain whitefish with fish in the 4 to 5 .lb range being common on some prairie lakes and reservoirs. The flesh of the lake whitefish is also more cherished by fish eaters than the mountain whitefish; a commercial market for Lake Whitefish has existed for years and as far away as cities like the city of New York have created a demand for this fish.

The lake whitefish spawns in the later part of the fall and early winter in November and December. Lake Whitefish are a long living species and can on average have a life span of up to 15 or 16 years of age. The current Alberta record for an angler caught Lake Whitefish is 11.lbs 10.1 ounces. They are fished for by commercial fishers on many lakes usually in the months of January or February every year so the numbers of larger fish for anglers can decline after this period of the fishing season. They are best fished for thru the ice using small jigs and spoons. Currently they are not commonly caught during the open water season by angling.

I think that this developing lake whitefish fishery will change over time as our knowledge of how to angle for this species improves. Lake whitefish are know to feed on a diet of small aquatic insects such as midge larva, pupa and other still water insect life that are common in many prairie lakes and reservoirs. Over time these feeding habits of Lake Whitefish will make them a prime target for the angler knowledgeable in fishing these types of fly patterns. Present day, most anglers that head to a prairie water body have pike, walleye or stocked trout on their minds, but there is a tremendous opportunity waiting to be explored and eventually the whitefish will also be a target in the focus of still water fly fishers.

Northern Pike

The northern pike is a great sport fish and in the minds of many an angler they are the primary species for the angling publics recreation over most the provinces hundreds of lakes. Its abundance and eagerness to take a lure any time of the year make the pike a sure bet for those that know its habits. If ever there was a fresh water predator designed for success on most of Canada's northern lakes it would have to be the pike. They are long lean and ready for a meal as they cruise the depths or skirt the weed beds in search of prey.

The fish thing that comes to my mind when I think of the novice and the pike is; don't stick your finger in a pikes mouth! All of pikes teeth, including the incisor's, are angled back toward the fishes throat. If you put your finger in the mouth of a pike and it closes in a bite, your first instinct is to pull your finger out, the problem is that this will magnify the damage that will occur and a nasty wound will result. As a young angler I had to learn this the hard way.

Pike like to ambush their prey and the best area of a lake to do this is in or around weed beds. They will also feed in open water areas if there are schools of fish for them to feed on. The first 4 pike that I caught were holding along weed beds near a boat dock on 3 different lakes. The boat docks are always kept free of weeds creating an open water area near the shoreline. Many lakes are choked with weeds in the summer months and it is hard for the shore angler to find a spot to cast a lure, boat docks were always my first choice when on summer holidays on a pike lake.

Pike are spring spawning fish and will usually start in May on shallow water areas of a lake. Many lakes have a spring closure for this reason. However, after spawning occurs they return to feeding actively and it is during this period of time when an angler can do well. The average size of mature pike makes them a prize catch for any angler and fish of around 10.lbs are quite common. The Alberta record for a pike caught by an angler was 38.lbs 0 ounces.

If you are fishing for pike there is a good chance that there will be walleye close by. These two sport fish tend to inhabit the same type of water on lakes across the province. The walleye is a major predator similar to the pike but more adapt at feeding in the dark. This is evident if you look at a walleyes eye; it is a silvery light sensitive layer that gathers light in low light conditions. Due to this sensitivity to light walleye will go deep in clear water lakes when conditions are too bright during the midday time period.

The life span of an adult walleye can range from 13 to 16 years in the south central part of Alberta. They will start to spawn in the spring around May and June in the main body of the lake or in an inflowing stream. After spawning the walleye becomes quite active and feeds regularly in the early morning and late afternoon – evening periods. Like pike they too like to hold near or in weed beds on lakes or at drop offs with a rocky bottom. They will take a moving lure with vigor but still baits are sometimes taken very lightly.

Throughout the province of Alberta there has been a major recovery management program for both pike and walleye. The walleye was the first fish species of the two to receive a no kill policy to recover collapsed populations on many of the provinces lakes. In recent years the pike has been added as a beneficiary of new management strategies to protect their numbers.

For many years both pike and walleye have been sought after for their excellent eating qualities, and large numbers of spawning size fish were harvested for the dinning table. It is hoped that once these populations recover to earlier numbers and sizes there will be new harvest rules to protect and enhance the fishery. You can still harvest fish in certain water bodies but you should bear in mind that taking more than you need will impact the fishery and affect your angling experience in the long run.

The annual fishing guide to regulations published by the Alberta provincial government has annual updates on the policies that are underway and under review for future management strategy. I find this part of the publication especially interesting and it helps me understand more about the resource that I have enjoyed so much and plan on enjoying into the future. Also in the regulations book there is an excellent illustrated guide to help identify all of the different sport fish in Alberta.

Every angler should make a point of educating themselves on identifying all of the different trout species, by doing so you will become a better angler and your efforts will help in the management of the resource. Some species of trout are quite similar to each other and I have known anglers that have fished for years and still could not identify some types of trout positively. Because of the environment that some trout live, their color will vary considerably and the lack of predominant features will confuse you.

A good case in point is the reservoir or lake brown trout, which are more silver in color than many other brown trout and they can appear similar to a rainbow trout as a result. The Ghost reservoir browns for example; there is no brown or golden yellow in their coloration. They have large black spots and a square tail and this is the only distinguishing traits that make them identifiable.

This inability to properly identify trout species can make management of the resource difficult. With creel surveys being used as part of the management practices throughout the country, the recording of wrong species in the creel survey data can throw a loop into accessing trout populations.

I know that some fisheries managers are using an identification test program to qualify anglers for participating in some fisheries management programs. This test method is a great way of making sure that fishers have the right knowledge of species identification before they head out onto the water to fish and record their catch.

I checked out the online fish identification test website to check it out a few years ago. The selection of photos of different species of trout can be an eye opener for those that are unfamiliar with some of the variety of color traits and body dimensions typical to different trout that inhabit our streams and lakes. The site is a great tool for educating anglers and a good way to test your know how.

I can understand that in future years, with management of different trout waters receiving special attention, this education program will become more important in our management strategy of the fisheries.

In recent years, one of the area fisheries biologists has teamed up with Trout Unlimited to study the use of selective harvest of certain species to promote the recovery of other trout species. In this particular case, the targeted species for harvest is brook trout and the two other trout species that are being promoted into recovery are bull trout and cutthroat trout.

The program is called the Quark Creek Project and in order for an angler to participate in the study, they have to pass a fish identification test to qualify. Since the program started, back in the early years of 2000, the results have been very promising. With large numbers of brook trout being harvested and the bull trout and cutthroat trout being released, the population numbers of bull trout and cutthroat trout have increased substantially.

This selective harvest program has also benefited threatened species on other area waters. In 1998, new regulations to protect cutthroat trout were applied to the Waiparous Creek. In the new regulations all cutthroat trout had to be released and only two brook trout could be kept for harvest. As a result, the numbers of cutthroat trout have increased substantially since 1998.

Prior to the new regulations on Waiparous Creek, the stream was dominated by brook trout, with only a few cutthroat trout being caught each season. However, at that time, the cutthroat trout were usually larger in size than the brook trout and more cutthroat trout were being harvested for the frying pan.

Artic Grayling: Typical to the northern part of the province, Arctic Grayling have been introduced to a number of area ponds and lakes.

Brook Trout: These pretty trout were stocked extensively on Alberta lakes and streams over the years. They are small in size compared to other trout species but what they lack in size they make up in numbers.

Brown Trout: This introduced European species of trout is notorious for its cunning and difficulty in capture. Brown trout have adapted well too many streams and lakes where it has flourished for years.

Bull Trout: A native species of Alberta trout.

Burbot: This unattractive fish is great table fair.

Cutthroat Trout: This native Alberta trout is common on many mountain streams and lakes.

Lake Trout: The lake trout is known to grow very big and it is common on many Alberta lakes.

Lake Whitefish: The Lake Whitefish is a very popular eating fish typical on many lakes throughout the province.

Rainbow Trout: The rainbow trout is one of the most sought after sport fish in many streams and lakes.

Rocky Mountain Whitefish: The mountain whitefish provides great angling for many fishers. It is abundant in many Alberta foothill and mountain streams.

Pike: Over the years, the pike has been a very popular sport fish in Alberta. This photo of an anglers catch was typical in years past; the fish is now under special management in the province of Alberta.

courtesy of Sports Scene Publications Inc.

94

Part Seven

Ice Fishing With a Fly or Jig

It is November 7 and over the last few days the temperature has dropped; as I look out of my window large flakes of snow are falling from an overcast sky. The water on the smaller sloughs and ponds has frozen over in the last few weeks and soon the larger lakes will ice up in the stillness of the night. For an angler this is the transition period between the open water fishing season and the winter ice fishing season. In the first weeks of December area lakes will be covered with a thick enough sheet of ice that an angler can walk to a chosen area of the lake and auger a hole down to the black water below.

For 4 or 5 months of the year Alberta lakes and reservoirs are covered with ice and the feeding habits of sport fish are slowed down by the colder water temperatures. For the committed angler that enjoys the sport year round, they are faced with an alternative method of catching fish thru a hole augured in the ice. As true Albertans we are not going to let a little cold weather and blowing winds discourage us from our leisure in the great outdoors. You may feel some what on your own in this endeavor until you make it to the lake and see other folks with the same idea.

The experience of trying to catch a fish from under the ice has a special allure, one can only experience it if their desire to do so is strong enough. If the interest is there, the routine of being prepared and going thru the process necessary to catch a fish in this manor will grow on you. Over time you find that the experience of ice fishing develops into an annual recreation that will get you out of the indoors when most people would consider the weather a major inconvenience.

Due to variable weather conditions from year to year the first ice up on the fishing lakes will vary. In our region we can usually look forward to being on the ice in the first part of December. When I say on the ice I am referring to walking on the ice. Despite rumors about when the ice is thick enough for an angler to walk safely on its surface I have learned over time and experience that better safe than sorry. On most lakes 4 inches of ice is adequate thickness to support any angler but on some area reservoirs that are exposed to high wind conditions a sheet of 3 inch ice can be broken up by high velocity winds that blow over its surface, so if you are on 4 inches of ice when the wind starts to blow consider my warning.

The Ghost reservoir to the west of Calgary is one such reservoir that can be dangerous early in the ice fishing season. I have seen areas of the lake with a section of broken ice caused by the wind in the month of December. I have fished the lake for a number of years and during early ice fishing trips during these early season days, I don't like to venture to far out onto the lake until there is 4 ½ inches of good ice. For driving a vehicle on the Ghost I wait until there is 1 ½ feet of ice at the lower end of the reservoir because some years there will be thinner ice at the upstream end of the dam than there is on the lower end.

I will go more into depth about ice fishing safety later on in this chapter but for starters let us look at some of the basic requirements for getting on the frozen surface. Ice conditions can make even the most experienced anglers nervous but once you understand ice conditions better and learn an early respect for winter lake ice you should have no problem making the right decisions for fishing on lake and reservoir ice.

Now that we have looked at the basic ice conditions for winter ice fishing let me direct your attention back onto some of the benefits of this type of fishing during the winter months. Fishing lakes and reservoirs provides an angler with the opportunity to fish different areas of a water body that they might not have the pleasure of doing in the open water season. If you don't have boat or other means of venturing out into a lake when there is open water, during the ice fishing season you do. All of the lake structure that you fish in the spring, summer or fall or wished that you did, is now available by simply auguring a hole and starting to fish.

One very important difference compared to the open water months of the year is that with the protective covering of ice on the lake the fish are hidden from open water predators, the fish will feed much closer to the shoreline. Areas such as shallow bays and points where fish avoid traveling during the day light hours of the open water season are in winter prime feeding areas. For lakes with deep drop offs the sport fish may be feeding in shallow water right along the shoreline, in a little as 2 or 3 feet of water.

Where you fish on a lake will depend on the type of fish you are after. Many sport fish will hold in deep water but will feed in shallow water. Ice fishers sometimes make the mistake of starting to fish over deep water right away when they could be doing well in shallow water. It is difficult to know right away where you should be fishing a lake during the winter but experience will guide you along.

Like most new comers to an ice fishing lake, the first thing you do when you get to the lake is look for areas where other anglers are fishing. Without moving in to close to their spots you can drill a few holes nearby and watch your neighbors as you fish. I have found that most ice fishers are generous with tidbits of helpful knowledge. Another sign of a good location can be holes that have drilled thru the ice on previous days. If you find a location where there are a lot of old augured holes there is a good chance they are there for a reason.

Recently, there have been a number of books published and available which provide bathometric maps of many of Alberta's fishing lakes. The maps show the contour of the lake shoreline and the different depths of the lake. These maps are a handy item to have in your tackle bag. Some anglers that fish lakes during the open water season make GPS records of where the different structure in the lake is located and they can use those records for finding the same spots in the winter.

Once you have established where you are going to drill your holes on a lake or reservoir you have to make sure that you have the right equipment to fish. For auguring holes thru the ice the most popular hand auger on the market still today is the Swedish auger. The Swedish auger comes in a range of sizes from 4 ½ inch to 8 inch. The small 4 ½ inch is generally used for small pan fish such as perch and the larger 8 inch is designed for landing larger fish such as lake trout and pike. A very common size for most ice fishers is the 6 inch auger for most average size sport fish.

When you are deciding on which size of auger that you should buy make sure that you consider the difficulty of having to auger an 8 inch hole compared to a 6 inch. Remember this basic rule, the larger the hole, the more effort that is required to get thru the ice. This can become especially important when the winter ice grows in thickness. If you are taking young children along on your ice fishing adventure you will have to auger a lot of holes.

If you are planning on doing some serious ice fishing annually, you may consider the option of buying a power auger. Power augers are expensive but if you do a lot of ice fishing you will be thankful of your purchase. What I found that was the most noticeable advantage of a power auger, is the ability to try more areas and depths on lakes, with out a second thought. With a power auger you can also auger a much larger size hole diameter than you can by using a hand auger. I can auger a 10 inch hole in 3 feet of ice in 30 seconds. Just make sure that when you are using either a hand auger or a power auger that you don't auger into the bottom of the lake. If you dull a set of auger blades even just a little, the performance of the auger will be altered and rendered ineffective.

As I previously mentioned winter conditions are very hard on fishing reels and line, many ice fishers chose ice fishing rigs for the winter months instead of using their open water tackle. Ice fishing rigs come in a variety of designs, but basically they are assemblies of wood and line that are built so that they don't get pulled into the augured hole when you catch a fish.

The line on an ice rig is shorter in length than that which you carry on a reel, sometimes only 50 feet. Fish that are caught in the winter are very lethargic and don't fight as vigorously as they do when the water is warmer. All of the fish caught on an ice rig are fought and landed by hand. The fish is played by letting it pull line thru your hands if it makes a run and hand lining it in when you feel less resistance. For very large fish this may be a bit tricky at times but it can be done. The nice thing about ice fishing rigs is that they are simply to build, use and stow away.

Anglers that prefer the feel of a rod and reel in their hands the new short length ice fishing rods are your best bet. Unlike a long rod, with a very short ice rod you can reel in a fish and stay positioned over the hole where you can see what is happening. I use just the butt section of my spinning rods when I ice fish, if the drag is set properly you can play a fish off of the reel without requiring the flex of a short ice fishing rod. With most of the smaller fish that I normally catch, I just hand line the fish up thru the hole without bothering with the rod and reel. If the fish is over 3 or 4 .lbs I will use the rod to land it.

In the winter months sport fish grow lethargic and they try to conserve their energy to make it thru until the spring on what little food is available. During the open water season there is plenty of insect activity and small minnows from the spring spawning season, but in the winter the food can be scarce and the hunt for it futile. With the water temperatures near freezing in the shallow areas of a lake sport fish do not need as much food to maintain their body weight when compared to warm blooded animals. It is nature's way of helping them to survive during the winter.

Presenting a fly at this time of the year helps if you have a little bait on the hook to entice a good bite. Some jigs can be fished without bait but for most of the ice fishing that I do I like to add a little bait if it is allowed, especially for still lines that you are not jigging. I suppose that the need for bait on my flies or jigs is related to the fact that much of the ice fishing that I have done is on waters that receive heavy fishing pressure. I have tried fishing just flies alone without bait but I found that the hits that I got were very brief and I didn't have time to set the hook. The only exception or alternative to the use of bait while ice fishing, would be when you are visually fishing a fly or jig.

If you are in an ice fishing hut or shack and you can see the bottom where you are jigging a fly, you can set the hook when a fish comes in for a bite. Fishing for Lake Whitefish is a good example; you have to be ready for a quick hook set when you are jigging for Lake Whitefish. But the conditions are not always ideal for this type of visual fishing so bait is going to be part of the sport for success.

For most fish that I normally ice fish for I like to use a fly, weight and a fixed bobber. This method has proven successful for rainbow, brown, brook trout and mountain whitefish. There are a few different ways that you can rig up your line to fish a fly but the method that I use the most is fishing two flies and split shot on the end of my line. You can either have your weight on the bottom of the line and the two flies up from it or you can tie on a fly at the bottom and then another about two feet up the line with a split shot in between the two flies. The second method allows you to fish your flies suspended off the bottom or 10 or 12 feet below the ice.

The bottom area is usually the best place to have your flies but under certain conditions fish will suspend and travel at different depths. On many lakes there is a thermo cline where the water temperature is slightly warmer than that above and below a given depth. Fish will sometimes hold in this warmer water and when they do, you should have your fly at the same depth. It is difficult to determine where the thermo cline is in a lake without the use of a temperature gauge or a sonar unit. Sonar units will pick up on a thermo cline if the sensitivity is adjusted correctly. For most anglers it is a matter of trial and error to find out at which depth the fish are.

When I decide at which depth that I am going to fish I lower my flies down the hole in the ice and then attach a fixed bobber to the line. On a fair weather day I will let the bobber rest at the edge of the hole on a little mound of snow or ice from the auger. When I get a bite the bobber drops into the hole signaling a hit and I have time to get to my line and prepare to set the hook with a light jerk of the hand. I watch the bobber dip until it is pulled under the water then I set the hook. You can also attach a small bell to the end of your rod tip to signal a bite if you like, but make sure that your rod is well anchored before you place your line down the hole. You should also remember to set the drag loose enough to allow a fish to run when hooked.

The use of suspended flies and bait on lakes with stable water levels is an effective angling technique when you fish the normal structure of the lake bottom but on reservoirs it can be a major challenge. Reservoirs have water levels that fluctuate daily if they are power reservoirs or over the winter if they are irrigation reservoirs. I find the irrigation reservoirs to be easier to fish than the reservoirs used for power generation. Daily fluctuation can make it difficult for sport fish to develop routine feeding habits.

The Ghost reservoir is a large reservoir located west of the City of Calgary, Alberta. It is a major hydro power facility that generates power throughout the day and holds back water at night. There is a fair lake trout fishery in the lake but the majority of sport fish are mountain whitefish with a small population of brown trout, brook trout and cutthroat trout. For the smaller trout species and mountain whitefish you have to fish close to shore to achieve any reasonable success during the winter months. This type of ice fishing often involves fishing steep banks that drop down to waters edge without any noticeable shelf or shoreline weeds where the fish can hold. The fish that feed on these drop offs stay very close to shore and are constantly on the move.

In these tough ice fishing conditions I like to fish very close to shore in a depth range of 2 to 16 feet on most days and occasionally I will set a line at 20 or so feet for fish that are feeding deeper than normal. This method of fishing the Ghost has proven quite successful over the years and I will usually catch a number of mountain whitefish and a few trout on a winter's day of fishing. The best bite activity is early in the morning to around 10.30 and later in the afternoon until just before dark.

I use small flies for fishing the Ghost and other lakes and reservoirs. Size 10 to size 14 flies baited with a single or double maggot works good. When you hook on a maggot make sure that you hook through the blunt end, just thru the skin so that you don't kill the bait. This will allow the maggot to wiggle for some time before the water temperature slows down the movement of the bait. Early in the season, fly patterns such as "the Brown Hackle Peacock, Royal Coachman" or similar green and brown patterns seem to perform the best. Later on in the season I like to use bright colored flies in orange, fuchsia and chartreuse.

Every lake or reservoir will require different fly patterns for the fish that occupy the water and trial and error is usually what is required until you know the water and which fly works best. For trout water, another effective fly pattern is the jig. There are a number of rubber jigs on the market today but the old fashion chenille and marabou jigs are still one of my favorites. They come with a lead weight near the head area of the jig which makes them sink fast and also it allows you to jig at various depths. This jigging action will often entice a bite from a trout that is on the prowl, so you have to be alert and ready to set your hook on a take.

In many cases trout will take the jig on the drop and the only way that you can detect a bite is by watching your line. If the line goes limp on the drop of the jig, this means that a fish has probably taken it and you have to be fast to respond. I like to use a very short jigging method that I learned from an angling buddy. He would sink his jig to a given depth and use very short jerks on his rod tip to give the jig an undulating motion that produced great results.

For the larger sport fish, like lake trout and pike, jigging is also the best approach for catching active fish. The jigs that you use for these larger trophy fish will have to be larger in size and will require a heavier weight on the jig head to keep you in touch with your jig. Here is where a rubber tail jig, like a curly grub or worm will add to the action that you may require too achieve a better result. These modern plastic baits also come in minnow imitations and other odd assorted wiggly creatures.

My favorite color of jig for fishing lake trout and pike is white. White jigs resemble the color of juvenile lake and mountain whitefish that are prime forage for pike and lake trout in Alberta reservoirs and lakes. I always like to start fishing with a white jig and if white does not produce the response that I expect, I will change color to fluorescent yellow, chartreuse or some other color. Where the use of bait fish is permitted, I like to add a minnow for bait on the jig hook. The added scent of bait will sometimes make the difference between success and failure, in getting the fish to respond.

When fishing for rainbow trout in stocked lakes, I use a small jig and a piece of bait to fish stationary for feeding trout. I rig my line with a small weighted jig hook with a chenille body and a marabou tail in hot colors such as florescent yellow, chartreuse and fuchsia, these colors work great for trout during the winter months. The chenille is tied over a body of wrapped lead on the jig hook shank so that there is no hard surface for the trout to feel when they come to bite, similar to a plastic tube jig.

I lower the jig, baited with a piece of worm for scent, down to the depth that I want to fish and then attach a fixed bobber to the line. The bobber is placed on the side of the hole or on a small piece of wooden lath lying across the hole, so that it will fall freely into the water when the trout first bites. Using a wooden lath bobber rest also helps centre your line in the middle of the hole, preventing the line from freezing to the side of the hole on cold days.

It is a good idea to use a small size bobber for this fishing method, a bobber that is just large enough to keep your fly and weight suspended when it is in the water is a good choice. A smaller bobber creates less resistance when a fish pulls on your bait and this will encourage them to be more aggressive on the take. I have found that needle bobbers work the best for this fishing method. They are more stable resting on the lath, especially if the wind is blowing.

To enhance the weight of your baited line, removable split shot come in handy. Removable split shot have small wings opposite of the gap so that you can squeeze them together when you want to remove your weight. This is a nice feature that allows you to make adjustments in the quantity of your required weight.

I have used this method with good success on brook trout and walleye as well. With walleye I prefer a slightly larger hook size and I use a small minnow for bait. The walleye will often bite very lightly, so you have to be watching your line closely. For soft bites I don't think that there is any fish more adept at lightly mouthing a baited hook than the winter walleye. Sometimes they will swim up to a bait and suck it in with little movement in the line to indicate a take.

I was fishing Crawling Valley Reservoir once on a late winter afternoon, in shallow water with about 6 feet of depth below the ice. The Chinook wind was blowing, not hard but steady as my fishing buddies and I tried to catch a few more walleye in our last hour of fishing. I had rigged up a wind jig on my line to help give my jig a little added action. The wind jig was a small piece of cardboard that I had fastened to my rod tip. The cardboard was shaking in the wind and gave the rod tip an erratic action that was moving my jig and bait.

On the surface of the water, where my line entered the hole, I was watching my line dart back and forth as I patiently sat on a 5 gallon pail. Suddenly the line went straight and stopped moving, I looked at my rod tip but there was no sign of the pull of a fish. I grabbed the line and slowly pulled up until I felt something solid on the other end, I set the hook. A moment later I landed a nice 3.lb walleye. The fish had bit my jig and bait without pulling on my line. If I hadn't been watching my line at the waters surface, I would have missed my chance of catching the walleye. This experience taught me just how subtle a walleye will take some baits during the winter months.

Winter ice fishing would not be complete without the use of jigging spoons to catch everything from Lake Whitefish, to giant lake trout and pike. This is the only time of year when I will use metal spoons or spinners to catch fish. Out of necessity, it is sometimes the only way for improving your catch average. Jigging spoons and lures come in a wide variety of colors, designs and sizes. Some of the more popular ones in our area are the buzz bomb, the Swedish pimple and the huge variety of spoons available for fishing mainly in the open water season.

The ice fishing lures made from metal are used to catch fish off of the bottom of a lake or reservoir. You let the lure sink to the bottom and then retrieve it up a foot or two before you start to jig. I'll tell you, it's a good way to help keep yourself warm on a cold winter's day. The flash and color of the jigging spoon will draw fish in for a bite when other forms of angling are not producing results.

Above Photo: Jerry Nielson with a 20.lb Ghost Lake trout.

For most of the spoons available for ice fishing you must have a swivel attached to the line to allow your spoon to spin and twist without twisting your line. I prefer spoons with a single barb less hook to facilitate the safe release of fish that you hook and land. Spoons can also be baited with smelts or bait fish if allowed. This added scent is a must, if you plan on

103

catching fish. Buzz Bombs seem to be the only bait-less lure that produce results without adding bait.

Part Eight

Ice Fishing Shacks or Huts

I had mentioned earlier that ice fishing huts or shacks are an important part of the ice fishing experience and for places like the Ghost reservoir, Spray Lakes and other area lakes and reservoirs it will make your outing that much more enjoyable. Not only will they provide you with a clear view down into the water when you're fishing shallow areas of a lake but they will also provide comfort when the cold winds blow.

Many of the area anglers that ice fish on a regular basis every year have shacks that they have built for the winter months, some with stoves and windows. There are relatively inexpensive fabric shelters with light frames that can be purchased for ice fishing. These fabric shelters are totally closed in and don't let any light in, which makes them great for visual ice fishing situations.

Portable Shacks

For portable ice fishing shack and shelters, you have to make sure that the hut is well anchored when you are not fishing in it, so that the wind doesn't blow it away. I can recall one humorous incident that occurred on Crawling Valley reservoir a number of years ago when my brother had to run like a track star to recover his shack, as it went sailing across the lake.

Portable shacks can be anchored into place by auguring a hole on the up wind side and installing a piece of drift wood, with water to freeze it in. If snow is available, you can dig the hut in and bank up snow along the outside. If you're lucky, it will be a calm day! However, if you take a chance and don't anchor your hut, know that when the wind comes up, you will have to scramble to stabilize the shack.

Smaller huts are designed to be more portable so that an angler can use them on many different lakes and reservoirs. My father built a few smaller style huts for fishing lakes other than the Ghost reservoir. He got the design idea from Jack Castle a local seasoned ice fisherman that has fished in this style of shack for years. The two huts that he put together are made of plywood and fabric. The shelters are about 4 feet wide by 5 feet long with a 4 foot ceiling. The basic lay out of the huts is a plywood floor with 12 inch holes on two corners and two end sheets of plywood that are hinged and fold down onto the floor. All of the plywood used is ½ inch. For the sides and roof a single sheet of heavy fabric is used.

When the hut is being assembled you lift the two end sheets of plywood up from the floor and use a stick that is the same length as the floor to jam between the two end walls at the ceiling. There is a small door on one of the end walls of plywood that allows easy access. Once the huts are assembled you can sit comfortably on a small seat inside the shelter and you have a clear view of the water below. The fabric used for the hut should be black and tightly woven to keep out the light. These huts are relatively easy to build and are very effective.

The first time that I fished from one of these smaller huts was a number of years ago on Gull Lake near the Town of Bentley. We were after the lake whitefish that were plentiful in numbers in Gull and they ranged in size from 3 to 4 .lbs and 20 to 24 inches in length. Having never fished the lake for whitefish before, I was ill prepared for the outing. I had a few small jigs and maggots but I didn't have any wire worms, in particular those that were colored bright red and yellow.

Those were the color of wire worms that nearby anglers were using when we arrived at the lake. A fellow next to the spot where we augured our holes was catching fish after fish with a bright yellow wire worm that had been tied on a size 8 jig hook. He was fishing in about 8 feet of water that was crystal clear and he could see the large whitefish come in and take his jig. Regardless of the lack of the right fly patterns we managed to catch a few large whitefish on some florescent jigs with maggots.

The size 8 jigs were baited and lowered to a spot just off the bottom of the lake, which was covered in a mat of weeds that had rested on the bottom earlier in the winter. The jigs were jigged, wiggled and spun in circles trying to entice a whitefish in to bite. When the large whitefish did come in it was all visual, you had to wait and watch for when the whitefish sucked in the jig before you set the hook.

As soon as the jig disappeared you set the hook and started playing your fish. The most important moment when you are trying to land any fish through the ice is when their head gets near the hole, you have to make sure that the fishes head is just starting to enter the hole before you make your final pull to extract the fish from the water. More fish are lost at this point in time than many anglers would care to remember. If you pull too soon the fishes head and mouth will get caught on the edge of the ice and you may lose your fish.

The spinning of a small jig is a technique that is not that well known among many ice fishers. My dad learned about it from Jack Castle when they were ice fishing together. The jig is dropped down to the right depth and then using your first or middle finger and your thumb you twist the line forward and backward in your fingers. This action imparts a spinning motion in the jig. When done with a wire worm on a curved hook it imitates a wiggling midge larva or aquatic worm. Both Jack and my father used this method when they were fishing small tear drop jigs of various colors.

Large Ice Fishing Shacks

Back in the early 90's my brother built a deluxe ice fishing shack for fishing the Ghost reservoir every winter. The shack is about 6 feet wide 8 feet long and 7 feet high. It has a bench on one side and a wood burning stove at the end and shelving across from the bench. The framing is 2 x 4 inch construction, with a plywood roof and ½ x 6 inch ruff cut spruce siding. The floor is also plywood with two 12 inch holes located in front of the bench. There are two windows, one on each side of the shack.

As you have probably guessed the shack is not light in weight. I would guess the shelter's weight at around 300.lbs, with the snow cleared off of the roof. There are two 2x6 inch removable runners that are used to tow the shack around on the lake. It is a cumbersome building but it is a real comfort to have on the lake when the cold winds blow.

A typical day's fishing on the Ghost involves arriving at an early hour on the lake, at which time; the first duty is to auger new holes in the ice. While the holes are being augured and cleaned of loose ice, a fire is lit in the stove and a pot of coffee is set to brew. The fishing lines are then prepared for the water. After the lines are baited and placed in the holes, a cup of morning coffee is poured and the day's fishing is underway. Around noon the mid day's meal is ready for the stove top and more coffee is hot and ready to drink.

By the end of the day the ice fishing shack's floor has been thawed free of the lake ice, if the shack is going to be moved to another location on the lake, it is at this time of the day that the moving of the shelter is carried out. Since the shack was first built, it has provided shelter on many an outing, weather conditions that would normally discourage most ice fishers are less of a concern. Since the comforts provided by the shack are available every winter, more time has been spent enjoying the sport and memories of good times are cherished.

Visual Ice Fishing

Visual ice fishing is by far the most enjoyable ice fishing experience. If you are equipped with a good shelter that blocks out the light you can get a clear view of what is happening down around your fly or jig. The water and available light have to be adequate for this watch and see method of catching fish. On many lakes and reservoirs the water clarity during the winter months is far better than during the open water season. One of the main reasons for better water quality is that there is no wave action to stir up the silt off of the shoreline or in the shallows. Also the light reflected by the snow on a lake will help illuminate the deeper water.

To fish by sight I prefer an area on a lake with weed beds that are lying across the bottom. These weed bed areas are good habitats for fish to feed in and by fishing your fly or jig close to the bed of weeds you are fishing the feeding zone. I have fished in depths of up to 12 feet with a clear view of my fly or jig near the bottom. In depths of less than 8 feet you have to be careful of any movement that you make when the fish come into the hook. Fish have a keen vision for anything above and the jigging a hand over the hole may spook them. When a fish comes in, move your jigging hand off to the side of the hole so that you can continue to jig without alarming the fish.

Jigging for fish that you can see will allow you to use flies and jigs without bait. The fish will not linger when they mouth a straight fly or jig without bait, however, because you can see the precise moment when the fish takes the fly you can set the hook. If you were fishing a line with a bobber, you rely on the fish being around long enough for you to get to your line and set the hook on a take. This is the advantage of using bait, once a fish tastes the bait they will continue to bite until you have a chance to catch them. Where it is possible I prefer to sight fish for trout, whitefish, walleye and pike, it is far more exciting to watch the action under the ice.

Above: An angler walks across the surface of the Ghost Lake in winter.

Above: A rather large Ghost lake trout is pulled from a 10" hole in the ice.

Part Nine
Area Fishing Destinations

Spray Lakes

Spray lakes is a long, narrow reservoir located approximately 95 km west of the City of Calgary. To reach the lake, you drive west of the Town of Canmore on Spray Lakes Road, up through "Whiteman's Pass" for about 20 km; just south of Goat Pond you'll reach the main dam. The majority of the trip is up a steep mountain road.

Whiteman's Pass was a common travel route for native Canadians, when moving to hunting grounds and a trade route into the Kootenay Valley. It got its present name when an expedition of white folks traveled through the pass in 1841. The James Sinclair party, which consisted of 23 families, left Fort Gary by Red River Cart's in route to the Oregon Territory, to establish British claims of sovereignty to the land. Sinclair and his group were guided along the route by a northern Cree Indian. I have traveled this pass quite a number of times over the years in a truck or car and it must have been quite a task to climb the 400 m elevation from the Canmore site with domestic animal carts.

The name Spray Lakes is a little confusing; the Spray is actually one lake. Prior to the creation of the two dams on the lake in 1949, there were three separate bodies of water. The uppermost body of water was called Jackson's Pond, from where a small creek drained down slope into the upper Spray Lake, which then drained via Buller creek into the Lower Spray Lake. The out flowing creek (Woods Creek) on the lower lake was a tributary to the Spray River. After the construction of the dam was completed and the reservoir was filled, the direction of the majority of flow leaving the valley was redirected from a southerly course, to a northern out flow. Most of the water leaving the reservoir does so via Goat Creek and the Rundle Canal through Canmore.

The Spray covers about 20 square kilometres under full storage capacity, with approximately 50 km of shoreline. Its maximum depth is about 65 m on the area of the old lower lake. The mean average depth is approximately 13 m. When the Canyon Dam road was open to the public, there was easy access to the west side of the lake, now you have to walk or ride a bike to travel the road. Most anglers that fish the lake use a boat.

Before the reservoir was built, the Spray valley was well known for its excellent cutthroat and bull trout fishery. In 1913, the recently established Banff Fish Hatchery (1917), created a subsidiary hatchery on the Lower Spray Lake to gather cutthroat trout and collect eggs for hatching. When the cutthroat trout would congregate in the spring of the year, at the mouth of Buller Creek, which flowed in from the Upper Lake, hatchery staff would net fish for processing.

The off spring of those fish were used to stock Marvel Lake and a number of streams and lakes in the area. The present day stock of cutthroat trout that live in Job Lake and that are used for brood stock, are descendents of those Spray Lakes cutthroat trout.

The construction of the dams and the flooding of the valley, led to the demise of the existing sport fishery. In an attempt to re-establish a sport fishery, the provincial Fish & Wildlife Division stocked the lake with approximately 400,000 eyed lake trout eggs between 1951 and 1954. To feed these newly introduced lake trout, they planted about 6.000,000 Cisco eggs in 1953. Further lake trout stocking programs would be carried out in the following years.

If you like to catch small lake trout and lots of mountain whitefish, this is the lake to do it in. There are plenty of them and they are easy to catch. In recent times, the average size that most anglers bring in is around 12" to 16", with an occasional larger trout being caught. Reports from area anglers that are knowledgeable of the Spray Lakes fishery, point out that the majority of larger lake trout caught on the Spray reservoir, are taken on the south end of the lake. This could be attributed to the nutrients flushed into the reservoir from most of the lakes major tributaries that enter from the south.

There are a few cutthroat trout to be caught as well; most are found close to the shoreline. The cutthroat trout are more common near the mouth of Watridge Creek, Smuts Creek, the Spray River and Bryant Creek but access to this part of the lake is limited to boat travel. The cutthroat trout and lake trout are taken on small lures and bait, including maggots and small fly hooks. The majority of anglers like to use smelts or pieces of smelt on lures and jigs, when angling for the lake trout.

It is presumed by fisheries managers that the lake trout in the Spray do not grow that large because of the lack of a good forage fish base. In a 1986 net survey, only 2% of 51 fish caught had fish in their stomachs. The lake trout feed primarily on aquatic insects, such as midge, may flies and caddis flies. In 1984, an experimental stocking of Opossum Shrimp (Mysis Relicta) were transplanted from the Upper Kananaskis Lake into the spray, in hopes that the shrimp would provide a viable food source for young lake trout and Cisco. The results of that stocking of shrimp were unsuccessful or yet undetermined.

Boats are nice to have for fishing the Spray but they are not necessary, you can still do well off the shoreline. The trout in the lake seem to prefer a little action with your offering, so try and keep some motion in your retrieve. They will take a still bait but you have to be prepared to wait for a bite. A piece of smelt or a whole one fished on the bottom has produce results. Remember to let the fish have some line before you set the hook.

A few good areas for fishing from shore are near the main dam on the east shoreline, for about 2 km south. The other well known spot for area anglers is on the west side of the lake across the main dam. At the end of the access road, you'll come to a gate. Park there and hike south along the Canyon Dam road until you come to the rock cut. Here the water drops off very close to shore and many a trout has been caught in this area.

There are five day use parking spots near the lake. A boat can be launched at two locations on the lake. One is at Driftwood Day-use area, on the east shore of the lake. Another is at the privately operated camping area on the west side of the lake. To get to the second boat launch, drive across the main dam and travel approximately 2 km south on the access road to the campground.

The Spray is a great destination for the ice fisher. The water is crystal clear in the winter months and you can see down to depths of 20', if you have a shelter to hide the light. This makes jigging a very interesting endeavor, with lots of action on a good fishing day. However, be prepared, the wind can blow like "Hell" and if it's cold already, the wind can end your outing. On the other hand, there are plenty of beautiful sunny winter days in the high country and the view is spectacular.

As the winter months progress, the water levels in the reservoir recedes, creating a steep slope of ice along the shoreline. You can buy inexpensive ice cleats for navigating this slope ice, if you don't already have them. These areas along the shoreline of the lake are very hazardous. Try and find an area with hard crusted snow cover to access the lake. The ice on this lake can get very deep in the later winter months, 3' or more. With the majority of trout on the smaller size range, a 6" ice auger is your best choice.

The Spray Lakes Fish Reef Project

In the late 1980's, TransAlta Utilites Corporation under took a major shoreline reclamation project on the Spray Lakes. The objective was to enhance the shoreline area of the lake which involved a clean up of old stumps, woody debris and re-seeding the slopes along the waters edge. Trout Unlimited approached the Canmore Scout Troupe with a proposal to utilize the stumps as fish habitat in the lake. The plan was to have the Scouts drill, cable and anchor the stumps together and then hire a helicopter to place these structures in the lake.

With limited time, resources and the shear magnitude of the project, the program was never completed. In 1997, while I was working on fish habitat enhancement on Canmore Creek, just down the road from the Spray, TransAlta asked me if I would be interested in completing the project. I like challenges and with the experience of managing a fish reef project on the Ghost Lake in 1989, I accepted the job. It wasn't until I surveyed the number of stumps that needed to be placed in the lake that I realized how big this job was going to be.

In total, there were 326 tree stumps to be submerged and they were spread out along a 4 km reach of the west shoreline. Pretty much all of them had been drilled for cable, by the Scouts and some had small concrete anchors attached or available. The first task "at hand" was to determine how much anchorage would be required to sink that much wood. I would have to conduct an experiment to figure out how dense the wood was after drying for so many years and how much concrete will be needed for a given volume of this dried wood. I knew that once the stumps were in the water and on the bottom, they would "water log" quickly, losing their buoyancy.

The next challenge was to decide on what method I would use to sink these stumps as reefs. They had to be positioned at the right depth and at a given location out from shore, where they would provide the best habitat for fish. Would a helicopter be the best choice for this project? It was going to be necessary to research all of my options for this project. I got on the phone and started to educate myself about all of the different choppers that could be used for such a task, what their lift capacity is - the cost per hour plus fuel, etc.

Then there was the weather up there. The Spray in well known for its unpredictable weather. The lake is located in a tight narrow valley, with weather fronts coming in from all directions, over the tops of the mountains. It can change within minutes up there. I was going to need a crew for this project and paying them standby was part of the project costs, if the weather turned bad. How about placing the reefs thru the ice in the winter months? After thinking about the idea for awhile, I determined that there had to be an easier, safer way of getting the job done.

On the west coast of BC, they have submerged a number of old ships for fish habitat and diving sites for sport divers. The ships go down by well positioned explosive charges penetrating air bulk heads in the vessels in a controlled manor. As the charges go off on the bow or stern of the ship, the vessel lists to one side or the ship goes down nose or tail first. This idea of using escaping air lead me to consider a custom made raft for sinking the reefs on Spray Lakes. If the raft could be built in a cost effective manor, its use would justify the expense.

In October of 1997, I completed an experiment to establish how much anchor weight I would need and I designed a raft to be used in the submergence program. To figure out how much weight would be necessary in the project, I took a small stump and measured the outer surface to determine the mass. By adding weights to the wood until it sank, I could determine the weight to mass ratio.

The stumps were then categorized into 3 basic groups; small, medium and large. Taking the average in each size group and measuring its mass, I could come up with an approximation of the total volume of wood for all of the selected stumps on the shoreline, which was to be used in the project. It was necessary to have all of the anchors poured in advance, because transporting them to the lake was a costly business.

With the results from the experiment, I calculated that the project would require approximately 40,000 .lbs (18,144 kg) of concrete anchors, to sink the 326 tree stumps to the bottom of the lake. With that much concrete being used, I felt that it was important that the design of the anchors included fish habitat requirements to further enhance the structures as a good environment for fish to find shelter and food in. The concrete structures would be kind of a mini-reef within a reef; that was the idea. The addition of fresh bio-mass, in the form of willows and limbs, would not only provide additional cover for fish but also attract aquatic invertebrates to the structures.

I designed the anchors to have a number of holes through their form so that the additional woody debris that would be added would help to stabilize the anchors during submergence and provide extra cover for fish. The LaFarge Cement Plant in the Town of Canmore agreed to assist with the pouring of concrete into the custom forms that I would need for the anchors. They could use excess concrete left over from contract jobs. This was a real bonus for keeping the project costs to a minimum. It was for a good cause! There are always a few anglers on staff to provide encouragement in such an endeavor. Darrell Snarud and his crew were a big help in the successful completion of the project.

To create holes in the body of the anchors, we used small pieces of corrugated drain pipe in the forms. These sections of plastic pipe were attached to garage pad re-enforcement wire mesh, which would add strength to the anchors. A length of re-bar was bent and placed in the forms so that steel loop was at the top of each anchor, for loading and attaching the structures together with steel cable.

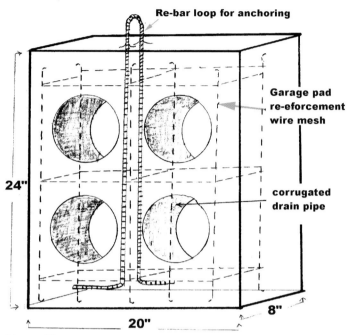

Re-bar loop for anchoring

Garage pad
re-eforcement
wire mesh

corrugated
drain pipe

24"

8"

20"

Above: The concrete anchor design used in the project.

The Anchors were poured at the LaFarge yard in Canmore

During the pour, the LaFarge truck drivers would work the concrete in around the mesh and pipe with a stick to prevent any "honey comb". The drivers finished the top of the concrete with a trowel.

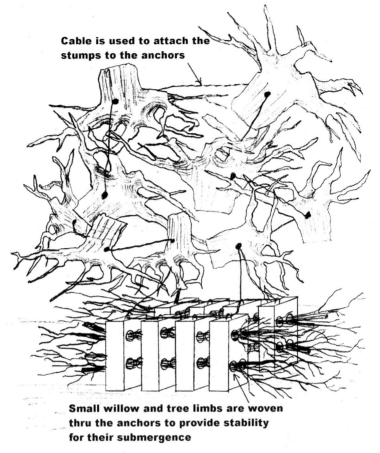

Cable is used to attach the stumps to the anchors

Small willow and tree limbs are woven thru the anchors to provide stability for their submergence

As an experiment, a number of anchors were built with 6 holes in the form. These 6 holed anchors later proved to be very effective when filled with willows, providing much more cover habitat. If I had the opportunity to be involved in another reef project, I would opt to use this design instead. The cost is a little more but the results can be justified. I originally had concerns that the concrete could not be properly poured in and around a 6 holed form but discovered that it can. With additional prodding with a tool, the concrete flows better and can be worked in around the plastic drain pipe.

The raft design was far more complex a challenge than the reef and anchor design. A raft that would carry a heavy load, be towed by a small boat, have the ability to tilt and dump it's load, then re-inflate for the trip back to shore, were the basic requirements. The craft would also have to be light enough for two people to lift and load it on a trailer. It took some careful thought but after a number of hours at the drafting table (desk) I came up with a design.

115

Above Photo: This is the cement form used to pour the anchors.

TransAlta Utilities had some really neat plastic pontoons in their yard on Rundle Canal in Canmore. I decided to incorporate these square bolt together units into the design, to provide flotation on the front of the raft and they would work as out riggers to provide lateral stability. Alex McFadden and the staff at the TransAlta office and shop also agreed to assist in the rafts construction, by ordering in materials and welding the frame.

Two members of my staff, Duncan McColl, David Mazzucchi and volunteer Doug Johnson of Cochrane, helped me build the raft over the following weeks. Doug is an instrument technologist at S.A.I.T. and was a big help in some of the calculations involved. Both Duncan and David were helping me out on the Canmore Creek Cutthroat Trout Project at the time and would soon be working on the Spray, helping me complete the project.

Once the design had been completed and the materials ordered in, it really didn't take that long to build the craft. Rick Cameron of TransAlta, did a great job on welding the light steel frame for the raft. If I was asked to put a dollar value on it, the price would have come in at about $1,700.00 in time and material. The cost of a helicopter big enough to lift one reef off the ground at that time was $2,300.00 per hour, plus fuel.

Raft being transported on a project trailer

In the first week of August 1998, the 191 concrete anchors needed in the project were transported to the three staging areas on the west side of the lake. From their location along the road, the anchors could then be moved down to the shoreline by a 4x4 Quad and project tilt trailer. I had chosen access sites where the use of a Quad and trailer would be safe and easy.

These little 4x4 machines are great in my line of work. You can move heavy rock and other materials with ease. The trailer that was custom built for such projects, has smaller wheels, with a low centre of gravity and when you come to a log laying across the trail, the trailer skids up and over it on the leaf springs and wheels. The tilt is used to load and unload heavy rocks and in this case concrete anchors.

On August 17th, the collection of materials and transportation of anchors to the shoreline assembly points began. Over the next week, root stumps were moved to the three main assembly sites with a boat. The stumps were rolled into the water and floated in a group by a boat tow. Fresh willow and tree limbs were collected from an authorized collection site and transported down to the assembly staging areas.

Anchors being assembled on the raft

Above: A reef assembly is completed on the shore of Spray Lakes.

Above Photo: A load of anchors has been assembled on the raft.

The early dim light of August 23rd outlined the rugged mountains along the lake's valley and promised good weather for the first day of the reef submergence project. There was no hint of a breeze and the lake was glass calm. It was a good day to be working in the mountains. Of all of the outdoor sites that I have worked in, this was the most picturesque. As I back my truck and trailer off on a side trail along the Canyon Dam road, I got out of my truck; at that moment I wish that I had a fishing rod in my hand!

Duncan, David and I unloaded the raft and carried it 40m down to the water's edge. The boats and motors had already been transported to site and were ready to go. I had a TransAlta, 14' aluminum with a Johnson outboard and my own 10' with motor as a back up and safety boat. I had made a ramp for loading the anchors on the raft; a wheeler truck was used to move the anchors up the ramp and onto the raft deck. We loaded the first batch of anchors onto the raft and started to thread the willow limbs thru the holes in the concrete.

I had pre-measured the depth and location of the submergence point on the lake, the day before and the site was marked with a flotation buoy. A GPS reading was recorded at the buoy for mapping purposes. My targeted depth for reef placement was 60' at maximum reservoir storage. This depth would allow for winter draw down, which would leave the reefs in about 40' of depth in the late winter and early spring. This location would be Staging Area One, Submergence Location One.

I was anxious to find out if the raft design was "up to snuff" so I decided on loading the raft to above full capacity for the initial trip out to the marker (Full capacity being the maximum load of anchors that would be required for each of the reef assemblies). To accomplish this, we loaded a number of stumps onto the raft along with the anchors. The main plan was to tow the stumps directly behind the raft to site when they were attached by the steel cable, thus reducing the amount of weight on the craft. The platform of the raft was only 10'x10'. For the test run I calculated that we had loaded approximately 2,600 .lbs of material on the raft and it floated like a charm. I pulled the load about 250m out to the marker buoy.

There was a 100' tow rope attached with an air line that could be controlled from the boat. The 100' rope tow was 40' longer than the maximum depth in which I would be working over, so I felt confident, from a safety perspective. The air line control allowed me to deflate the bladder in the back of the raft, for submergence and an auxiliary air storage tank in the boat held enough air to re-inflate the raft for the trip back to shore.

The tow out to the mark buoy was accelerating with excitement. The raft pulled like a dream and the small boat motor hummed with determination. I picked a spot about 50m from the marker to sink the first reef. I did a circle turn to position the boat upwind and I connected the release valve to the air line. I checked my watch and started to bleed the air from the raft. As the next minutes waned, the raft slowly started to tip, lifting the pontoons at the front of the raft out of the water. At 4 minutes 20 seconds and with the raft at about a 45 degree angle, the load came slipping off and the raft went shooting ahead in a plunge. It worked!

Above: Most of the raft is submerged just before the reef slips off into the depths of the lake, in approximately 60 feet of water.

As the reef slides off of the raft, the raft plunges ahead

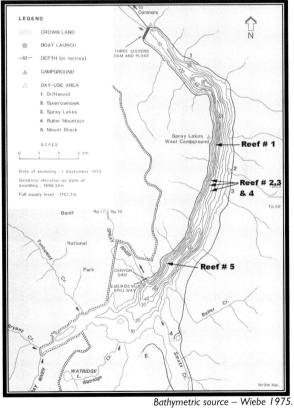

Bathymetric source – Wiebe 1975.

The Ghost Reservoir

The Ghost Reservoir is located approximately 40 kilometres west of the City of Calgary. The dam was built in 1929 by then Calgary Power Ltd. The reservoir covers approximately 11 square kilometres of surface area, 32 kilometres of shoreline and a maximum depth of about 30 metres, right next to the dam site.

The Ghost Reservoir was named after a main tributary river that enters the lake from the North. The Ghost River received its name after local Indian legend told of a Blackfoot ghost being spotted wandering the shoreline of the river, collecting skulls of fellow warriors, killed in battle with the Cree Indians. The river had originally been named on an 1860 map by the explorer "Palliser" as the "Deadman River".

There is probably some connection between the two names.

It is interesting to note that in 1988-89, when TransAlta Utilites Ltd., drew down the reservoir to do some renovations on the main dam, an old Indian camp was revealed in the area where the Bow River and Ghost Reservoir joined.

I was ice fishing with a friend, Ralph Tait, in 1989, when he told me that he had discovered quite a number of tee-pee rings on an exposed bench, just up from the old river channel. He took me to the site to show me.

There were rocks placed in circles with about a 12' diameter, these stones were originally used to secure the outside perimeter of tee-pees to the ground. There were some that were well bedded into the ground level, which indicated that the camp had been used for some number of years by the occupants.

With a little imagination, one can speculate that this nearby camp's location may have some bearing on the old Indian legend. In any case, the historic site now lies below the waters of the Ghost Reservoir.

Presently, the sport fishery in the lake is under utilized for a water body of its size, located so close to a major population of sport anglers. Anglers fish the Ghost Reservoir year round, with the majority of fishers visiting the dam to ice fish during the winter months.

The impoundment has a population of lake trout and mountain white-fish, with limited numbers of brown trout, Lake Whitefish, cutthroat trout, brook trout and bull trout. The Ghost Lake was stocked with both rainbow trout and cutthroat trout during the 1930's, 1940's and one stocking of rainbow trout in 1950.

The rainbow trout stocking program was unsuccessful and no con-firmed reports of rainbow trout being caught in the late 1950's were recorded. Some of the area long time anglers cannot recall the event, so we can probably determine that the trout did not survive through reproduction on any of the Ghost Lake tributaries.

Glenbow Archives NA-4477-56

Above: Site of Ghost Dam and hydroelectric power plant, July 1928 (Ghost Plant), Cochrane area, Alberta

Glenbow Archives NA-2924-15

Ghost River bridge, Ghost River, north of Cochrane, Alberta 1927-28

Above Photo: Ralph Tait stands inside one of the Tee-Pee rings exposed during a 1989 draw down of the Ghost reservoir.

Lake trout were stocked in the late 1940's and once in 1952. Although it is assumed that there is natural reproduction of lake trout in the Ghost Reservoir, it has been accepted that the survival rate of lake trout to maturity is limited. At this time, no studies have been conducted to back up this claim.

The majority of lake trout that are caught each year by Ghost angler's, are small in size. I have visited with a number of successful anglers over the last 20 years, while on the lake and their catches normally consist of lake trout in the 30 cm to 40 cm size range. This harvest of immature lake trout probably has a negative impact on reproductive activity as well.

The most productive fishery for Ghost anglers that are intent on catching fish is the mountain whitefish fishery on the lake. The reservoir has been and is a very popular spot for catching mountain whitefish along the shoreline. Along with these catches of whitefish, occasionally a brown trout or lake trout is landed. On rare occasions a brook trout, cutthroat trout or lake whitefish is also hooked thru the ice. Bull trout are very rare.

The brown trout fishery in the lake is very unproductive. There may be some spawning that takes place in the Bow River channel between the Ghost and Horseshoe Dams, or up the Ghost River system. However, the majority of browns in the Ghost are most likely "wash downs" from the upper Bow River system.

In the late 1960's and early 1970's, cutthroat trout were numerous on the upper end of the Ghost Lake. When I was shore fishing that part of the lake on a regular basis, back then, I would see schools of these cutthroat trout swimming close to the shoreline, just a few metres below the surface. We would catch these cutthroat trout by casting a worm about 3 to 4 metres out from shore and waiting for a bite, or casting a spinner just as a school of trout approached.

I am not sure where these cutthroat trout came from; I have been unable to track down any stocking records after the stocking in the lake that took place in 1949. The cutthroat trout that were caught at the time were all approximately 14 inches in length and very thick and deep in body confirmation. After examining their stomach contents, it was apparent that the fish were feeding primarily on small invertebrates, such as midge larva, water boatman, leeches and snails.

There is presently a movement afoot to have the Ghost Reservoir stocked with cutthroat trout, to increase the quality of the shoreline fishery on the lake. Whether the movement's goal will be successful is yet to be determined.

Angler Ron Darby holds up a nice lake trout from the Ghost Lake.

Phantom

of the

Ghost

Photo by
Mike Sturk

Phantom of the Ghost – By Guy Woods
(This article first appeared in "Western Sportsman" magazine in 1987)

I walked slowly along the north shore of the glass calm Ghost Lake reservoir. Reflections of the lake's wind blown shorelines reminded me of a Group of Seven landscape painting of a rugged, lonely island on the Great Lakes.

I was headed for a narrow channel in the lake, just down from where the current of the Bow River disappears into its depths.

I had learned of the spot as a boy. A neighbor told my father of the tremendous lake trout fishing to be had there, and after promising to keep the location to ourselves, we were guided to the secret spot. When we got there, we discovered quite a crowd of anglers.

That was nearly 20 years ago. Since then, the fishing spot has grown rather popular and the quality of fishing declined. But something kept a few keeners returning year after year – "a coal that keeps the fire burning" – the desire to catch a once-in-a-lifetime trophy fish.

It wasn't a blind ambition either; certain events had convinced some of the local anglers that some very large lake trout inhabited the Ghost's waters. Several trout of over 25 pounds (11 kg) had been taken from the lake.

As I topped a high ridge just west of the point where I fish from, I spotted a light blue Chevy pick-up. It belonged to David Baiers of Cochrane, another regular angler at this spot on the lake. David is a good natured angler whom has gained knowledge of how to fish this lake's waters; that comes only with experience.

My system for fishing the lake varies slightly from Dave's, but the basics, such as bait, are the same. To me, a sure sign of a confirmed lake fisherman is a highly personalized system of fishing. If you spend a considerable time at the end of your rod, you have to believe in what is on the end of your line.

Dave and I bait our hooks differently, but we use the same type of bait. *Osmeridae*, more commonly known as smelts, are the only dead bait fish, besides herring, that are legal to use on the lake, back in those years.

Once our lines were cast and brought tight to the waters surface, we were ready and waiting. With this type of angling, that is 99.9 % of the sport; "waiting for a bite".

Time slows when you are waiting for a bite. You acquire a heightened sense of awareness. A merganser cutting the glassy surface or a swarm of tiny midge flies hovering low over the water, nothing passes without your inspection.

Suddenly the silence was broken by Dave's voice.

"I gotta bite."

"Come on, take it again."

"GOTEM!"

The arc in Dave's rod indicated a small trout – small for a laker!

The bank we were fishing from was a steep, black shale slope. It made landing a fish a task, so I grabbed my long-handled net and offered to net the fish for him.

When the trout broke the surface, seven metres from the shore, I guessed it to be about 20 inches (50 cm) in length and 1.5 pounds (680 g) in weight. I dipped my net into the water and was watching the trout come in just below the surface when something spectacular happened.

A large, lone shadow sprung from the depths. I straightened from my bent-over position as a flash of silver and a huge tail broke the surface of the water and in a split second was gone.

"Rrrreeeeee. . ."

The sound of the drag on Dave's reel screamed with submission. I looked up to see a face, mouth agape, with the same look of astonishment that I felt.

A big trout had seized Dave's laker and was taking his line with it as it headed for the dinner table. I was dumbfounded. The size of the trout had left me speechless.

"Holy Jeece."

"Oh, man."

"Did you see the size of that thing."

David asked.

I nodded.

"That tail was at least 12 inches (30 cm) across!"

Dave's rod was still doubled over as the fish continued its run. The scream of his reel's drag suddenly ended. The fish was gone – the big fish that is. The smaller laker was still on the line. Dave reeled it in and an almost lifeless trout came to the net.

We discovered a large, horse-shoe pattern of teeth marks across the middle of the small fish, where the giant laker had clamped down on it.

During the next few years, I spent many hours on the lake. I caught some big trout, but nothing in comparison to that phantom trout Dave had on the line. I did, however, have some close calls with giant trout that taught me valuable lessons.

I learned through experience that large lake trout caught in the Ghost could not be horsed in using heavy line. I have broken 20 pound (9 kg) test line learning that lesson. The trout in the Ghost are unlike any lake trout I had ever caught. I was convinced that because of the shallow depth of the lake and the oxygen rich waters fed by the Bow River, that these trout were unique. For lake trout, they were tremendous fighters.

I once took a friend of the family fishing on the Ghost. He was an old timer who had once worked with my grandfather. Scotty loved to fish and he spent much of his free time fishing for salmon near his home on the west coast. When I handed him a rod equipped with a reel dressed with 20 pound (9 kg) test line, he laughed and asked, "What are we going fishing for, sharks?"

I laughed and replied, "I don't know, I've never had the opportunity for a close look. They've always broken my line."

Scotty could not believe that such heavy tackle was necessary on a small lake like the Ghost. To make a long story short, Scotty hooked into a big laker that afternoon. When he was just about out of line that he had given up to the trout, he tightened his drag until the line snapped. With a surprised look on his face, he exclaimed, "I've caught 30 pound (14 kg) salmon that didn't pull like that."

The largest laker I've taken from the Ghost was a 39 inch (1 m), 29 pound (13 kg) trout I caught in 1984. This catch was more of a stalk than a chance occurrence. I say this because I had the fish on my line two days before I actually caught it.

It was a windy spring day and I had decided to try fishing a new area of the lake. The place drew my attention because of the deep water within casting distance from shore.

Arriving at the spot late in the afternoon, I baited by hook and cast out into the lake. By watching the tightness of my line, I could tell when my bait hit bottom.

My line had just reached bottom when it began moving out into the lake. I pulled up the slack and set the hook. The fish started gathering speed as it pulled my 17 pound (7.7 kg) test Trilene line out into the lake.

The trout had taken nearly 150 metres of line off my spool when suddenly it stopped. My line went slack. I tried to pull up the slack but I could feel only the weight and possibly the bait on the end. I decided to leave it right where it was, hoping that the big laker would grab it again.

After two hours of waiting, I finally grew impatient. I reeled in my line to find the bait still intact. I spent the rest of that afternoon hoping to have another crack at the fish, but nothing happened. It was the same the following day, a Thursday that I struck the jackpot.

That afternoon was different from the previous two days. The wind blew hard from the east, crashing large waves on the rocks. Because of the head wind, it was difficult to cast my bait out onto the lake. It wasn't until my third try that I finally managed to get what I considered a good cast.

I had re-wrapped my spool with 14 pound (6.3 kg) test Stren line that night before. I had come to the conclusion that it was better to have a lot of light line rather than a heavier test and less yardage. If I had another crack at the big one, I didn't want to take any chances.

An hour passed. The chill of the wind made the waiting uncomfortable. The ice had left the Ghost a month earlier, but the icy waters of the Bow River had kept the lake's water temperature around the mid-40's Fahrenheit (7 c), a temperature range where lake trout become active.

It is really a game of chance with the giants that live in the lake. They may feed only once every week or two, depending on the size of their last meal.

Some large trout I have taken out of the lake have had nothing in their stomachs. It's when the fish are in this state that they can fall victim to anglers bait.

I was day-dreaming when I noticed my line slackening, so I reeled in a bit. It kept getting slack and I kept reeling it in. It stopped. My rod tip jerked forward as the fish turned and started a run with the bait. I set the hook with a solid yank. This only increased the fish's speed. I made some fine-tuning adjustments on my drag and let the fish work the line out into the lake, all the while pulling a 180 degree arc in my 10 foot (3 m) rod.

It was hard trying not to smile when I knew that at any second something could go wrong and I would loose the big trout.

The fish took nearly 150 metres of my line in a non-stop run. The line hung above the surface of the lake about 35 metres out before entering the water.

I was worried that a power boat might speed past and break my line with its prop. Fortunately, it was a weekday and there were only a few boats on the Ghost.

After the first long run, the laker stopped to try and free itself from the hook. Then it made another short run of about 25 metres. I began to worry about my limited supply of 200 metres of line; I was down to the last 25 metres.

When the fish finally gave up some slack line, I knew I had him. It took around 45 minutes to bring the laker in close enough for a look. At first glance I knew it wasn't the same phantom trout I had seen a few years before, but I certainly wasn't complaining.

When the fish finally came to the net, I was overcome by a feeling of relief. The corners of my mouth spread in an arc from ear to ear. All the time I had invested in Ghost Lake had me holding my once-in-a-lifetime trout. It was a just reward.

I never did catch that phantom trout that bit into Dave's small lake trout a few years earlier, but I haven't given up trying.

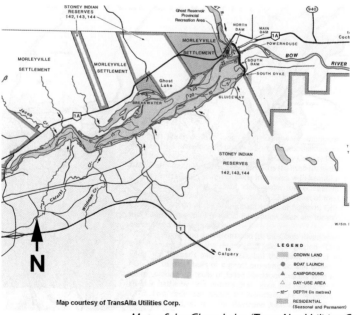

Map of the Ghost Lake (TransAlta Utilities Corp.)

Barrier Lake

Above Photo: Looking down on Barrier Lake Reservoir.

I stood on the shoreline as the boat backed down the ramp. It was mid September and early enough in the morning that the lake was glass calm. I looked out onto aqua-blue surface for any rising trout. It was a good start for a morning fish on the lake!

Eric Schulman and I were headed to the upper end of the reservoir, where the Kananaskis River has created a delta of shallow water with a lakebed that slowly tapers down into the depths. The nutrient that enters Barrier Lake from the river enriches the food supply for trout, especially brown trout, which was our primary target for that day.

After we stowed our gear in the 16' outboard, Eric fired up the 60 horse four stroke and steered the craft out into the main lake from our launching bay. Four stroke engines are so nice and quite; you could hear the water beating the bow of the boat as we glided along the near side of the lake's shoreline. It was a good time to enjoy the majesty of the Rockies and recall hunting forays into the adjacent valleys years earlier.

Some hunting buddies and I had set up a hunting camp on the far shore of Barrier back in the late 1980's and I recall the bear troubles we had during the night. A small black bear had a routine of raiding our camp at night creating an air of uneasiness for a group of tired hunters trying to catch some well earned sleep. It wasn't until old stinky stepped in that we finally resolved the problem.

Old stinky was a scarecrow that I fashioned out of some smelly cloths created from chopping wood and climbing mountains on the first day of the hunt. I dressed up a cross made from some dead willow trunks, draping the shirt and pants to look like a human standing night watch, complete with my hunting cap. I placed old stinky on the main trail that we suspected the black bear was using to visit our camp. That night, I was awakened from my sleep by what I thought was a loud snort. After that we all slept in peace.

As the boat approached the delta at the upper end of the lake, I pointed to an area that both Eric and I had ice fished the previous winter. Eric nodded with confidence and he started to report the depths showing on the boats depth finder as we started to slow down.

Over the years, the location where the Kananaskis River enters the Barrier has changed, leaving a series of old channels in the lakebed. Our days plan was to explore these channels and hopefully learn a little more about which areas the trout preferred. The first stop was about two hundred metres from where the present day channel enters the lake.

We had both noticed a number of rising trout in the delta area as we approached from the north-east. These tell tale signs of feeding trout helped elevate our enthusiasm and helped confirmed our plan for the day. There were a few good rings on the surface which indicated some larger trout or whitefish were on the feed.

The boat motor was shut down and lifted out of the water to allow the craft to glide ahead silently. I focused on the surface, trying to find out what the rising fish were interested in. The only bugs that I could see on the surface were small midges, light in color and about a size 20 hook length. As the boat came to a stop and started drifting, the trout started to rise more often. They were coming up over the shallow areas of the delta, where the lake bed was covered with aquatic weeds and some surface sedge was breaking thru the water's surface.

As we drifted down into a pod of rising fish, we anchored the boat and started to set up our lines. I had one fly pattern that closely resembled one of the midges that I had spotted, so that was my choice of fly pattern to start with. Eric opted for a small nymph bead head pattern that he had tied on his line. Before long we were both casting at the rings left in the surface after a fish had risen.

It's interesting to note how quite things are when two anglers start casting to rising trout, it must me the level of concentration and anticipation that ensues. No one says anything until "Had a Hit" or "Got One". Eric was the first to break the silence with "Fish On" – "A Good One"! It was a perky brown trout that before long came into the net. It was a nice brown trout of about 12 inches.

The interesting thing about this trout was its lack of red spots, typical to most brown trout that you catch in the area. I have caught a number of brown trout with no red spots over the years and I suspect that they may have some Scottish blood in them. Prior to the introduction of German brown trout in many area water bodies, the Banff Hatchery stocked Scottish Loch Leven brown trout. Loch Leven's are easily identified by their lack of red spots that are typical on the German variety.

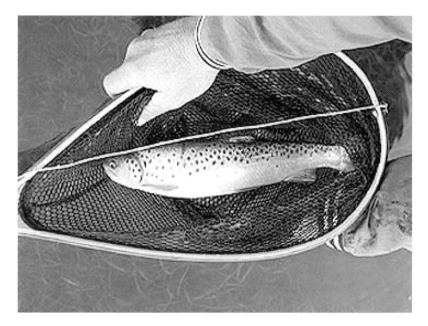

Above Photo: This is the brown trout that Eric hooked into.

When I was a boy, fishing the Bighill Creek in the Cochrane area, many old timers that had spent most of their lives in Cochrane, would ask me; "Have you caught any Loch Levens in the creek?" I wondered for years what they had meant by this term. Was it a special type of trout that lived in the waters of the Bighill Creek? Little did I know at that time that they were talking about the Scottish brown trout that had been stocked there back in the 1920's.

It wasn't until years later that I put the puzzle together. After reading a 1930's, Dominion of Canada fisheries report, from the Banff Trout Hatchery that was first built in 1917, I learned that Loch Leven trout had been stocked in both Bighill and Dogpound Creek with limited success. This strain of trout had also been stocked in other area waters but it is hard to verify this information because the name of the strain and trout supply source for the Banff hatchery are listed but the stocking list just points out the species and where it was planted.

It could be that some of the genes of the Scottish brown are still out there. Every now and then you may catch a long distant relative that displays the Scottish brown trout's characteristics. I have also caught brown trout with no red spots on the Bow River in years past. Now I can add Barrier Lake to the list of potential sources of this rare trout.

It wasn't long after Eric's catch that I had my first trout on. It was a slightly smaller brown trout and it displayed the typical red spots commonly known in their appearance. The small trout had taken my size 20 midge pupa that I was fishing right in the surface film.

We hooked a few more trout in that location and then we both agreed that it was time to explore a few other areas in the delta and on the main lake. As it turned out, by the end of our day's fish, all of the trout that were caught were delta brown trout and a few mountain whitefish. The larger trout that were caught were in the 12" – 14" size range. What they lacked in size, they made up for in their strength and good form.

The Barrier Reservoir was first built in 1947 on the Kananaskis River. It is approximately 19 m deep just southwest of the main dam and over 23 m deep further up the lake, which leads me to believe that there was a small lake present before the dam was built.

I have ice fished the main lake near the dam and found that it is a great area to catch a lot of mountain whitefish. You have to fish relatively close to shore, in about 4' to 20' of water. However, be prepared for the wind! With the tight mountain valley bordering the shoreline of the lake the winds intensify as they pass through, creating some very extreme wind conditions. It is a good lake to have a portable ice fishing shack with you, to help break the wind and allow you to look into the depths as you fish.

It is my opinion that a stocking of lake trout would do a great deal to improve the quality of the fishery on Barrier. There are plenty of whitefish for lakers to forage on and I'm confident that lake trout would thrive in the deep cold waters of Barrier. There are said to be a few bull trout in the lake but I have yet to catch one. A stocking of bull trout would also enhance the fishery as well.

Kananaskis Lakes

For years, the Kananaskis Lakes have been the primary destination of area anglers that love to fish for lake grown rainbow trout. Both lakes have been stocked since the 1950's as a "Put Grow and Take" rainbow trout fishery. This translates into fisheries managers planting the lakes with small rainbow trout that grow to a catch-able size and then are meant to be caught and possibly harvested by sport anglers. After all, rainbow trout only live until approximately 6 or 7 years. For those anglers that are catch and release, these lakes were also a very popular fishing spot.

In the early 1990's, interest bloomed in protecting the native strain of bull trout that inhabited the lower lake. There was also interest developing since the 1980's in re-establishing the native cutthroat trout in the lower lake. The cutthroat trout was once the predominant species of true trout (non-char) that was present in the lower lake.

In 1913, the Dominion of Canada Parks department commissioned a study of fish species in Banff's area streams and lakes. A Mr. Vicks reported that Lower Kananaskis Lake contained "the finest cutthroat trout in the mountains" and that they were the fish supply depot for the Morley Stoney Indians. It was reported that the cutthroat trout would stack up below the Kananaskis Falls, at the inflow to the lower lake in the spring of the year, to spawn.

There is no doubt that when the lakes drainage was modified to accommodate the power generation system built in 1932 on the upper lake, the cutthroat trout had no place to successfully spawn and reproduce. The lower lake power plant was built in 1955.

In the early 1990's, when I was Fish Habitat Chairman of the Jumping-pound Chapter of Trout Unlimited, our group of volunteers assisted in the bull trout study on Smith Dorrien Creek, a spawning tributary for bull trout on the lower lake. It was amazing to see the huge bull trout that were being trapped and tagged near the mouth of the creek. A number of bull's were near 30" in length and approximately 6 to 7 .lbs.

Photo: From Left; Dave Carles, Gary Gilland, Garth Bruno and Fisheries Research biologist Craig Mushens, holding a Kananaskis bull trout from the lower lake.

Bull trout populations in the Lower Kananaskis Lake had declined in numbers from approximately 11% in the mid-1950's to 2% in the mid-1980. By 1992, there were only 60 spawning bull trout observed in Smith Dorrien Creek. With special protective regulations that were recently brought to pass, the study was directed at monitoring the trout's recovery.

I am happy to report that since my involvement in the program in the mid 1990's, the bull trout population in the Lower Lake has increased substantially. The Lower Lake bull trout are a magnificent fish and they are a real trophy catch that has to be released, which is also very gratifying.

Above Photo: Angler Darryl Downs attempts to net a Lower Lake bull trout with a very small net. In the end, he succeeded.

The Kananaskis Lakes have undergone some major management changes in recent years. The once popular rainbow trout fishery in the Upper Lake is dwindling away into history. In the later part of the 1990's, it was determine by provincial fisheries biologists that an attempt to create a trophy bull trout fishery in the Upper Lake would be a good idea and it would fit into the push for the creation of native species fisheries in the area. Despite protests from many area anglers that had been enjoying the rainbow trout fishery in the Upper Lake, the management policy went into effect.

The plan was to introduce bull trout into the Upper Lake, along with a native strain of cutthroat trout. The rainbow trout stocking program was brought to a halt. Once the protected bull trout was stocked, a new regulation to prevent the use of bait, while angling on the lake, was put into law. This change embittered a number of regulars to the lake and as a result, the fishing pressure on the Upper Kananaskis declined.

You can still catch fish on the lake during the winter months but you will have to work a little harder in doing so. This entire program ended the only substantial lake rainbow trout fishery in the Bow River drainage basin, outside of the Banff National Park. There are plenty of high mountain lakes to catch cutthroat trout in, but you'll have to hike into them.

There is still a reasonable rainbow trout fishery on the lower lake, despite attempts to establish a cutthroat trout fishery by a stocking program. It was thought that the rainbow trout that were previously stocked in the lower lake didn't have a spawning area. However, this has been proven wrong.

In 1995, I received a phone call from a fishing friend, Bary Bryant of Cochrane. Bary, along with his wife and family had been camping along Boulton Creek, a small tributary to the lower lake. He told me that he had seen some huge rainbow trout spawning in the creek on the May long weekend. I decided to take a drive up to the creek the following weekend to see for myself.

When I got to Boulton Creek, it was in freshet, the water was high and discolored from the run-off. However, I did spot a huge rainbow trout in the creek that was in spawning color and I also identified some redds (trout egg nests) in the shallower water. The creek was definitely being used for spawning by the Lower Lake rainbow trout.

I contacted the regional biologist for the province the next day to tell him what I had witnessed. His comments were that it was probably insignificant number of rainbow trout and most likely had little effect on the lake's rainbow trout population. I mentioned that with no protective regulations to prevent harvest of these trout during the spawning run, I didn't think that this helped any. As I write this in 2007, there is still no protection for this run of rainbow trout on Boulton Creek.

The name Kananaskis, was given to the lakes by explorer Captain Palliser in 1858. He named the lake after a native Indian, Joseph Kin-oh-ah-kis. Indian legend has it that Joseph recovered from an axe blow to the head in a fight at the confluence of the Kananaskis and Bow Rivers. The word "Kin-oh-ah-kis" also translates from the Stoney Indian language into "meeting of the waters".

The Upper Lake is the deepest, with a maximum depth of 108 m on the south-west area of the lake. The Lower Lake drops to approximately 42 m at the mid-point area of the lake. During the early fall of the year, both reservoirs are brought to maximum level to supply power throughout the

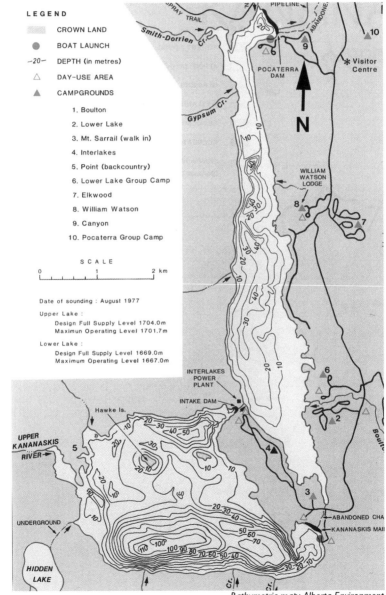

LEGEND

    CROWN LAND

●   BOAT LAUNCH

−20−   DEPTH (in metres)

△   DAY-USE AREA

▲   CAMPGROUNDS

    1. Boulton

    2. Lower Lake

    3. Mt. Sarrail (walk in)

    4. Interlakes

    5. Point (backcountry)

    6. Lower Lake Group Camp

    7. Elkwood

    8. William Watson

    9. Canyon

    10. Pocaterra Group Camp

SCALE

0   1   2 km

Date of sounding : August 1977

Upper Lake :
    Design Full Supply Level 1704.0m
    Maximun Operating Level 1701.7m

Lower Lake :
    Design Full Supply Level 1669.0m
    Maximum Operating Level 1667.0m

Bathymetric map: Alberta Environment

winter months. As a result, by late winter, the levels in both lakes are very low and you have to hike down a steep bank to get onto the surface of the lake to ice fish.

Extra care should be given when you traverse these banks, part of the banks are still covered in ice that slopes at a steep angle, creating hazardous conditions. Snow can hide fractures as the ice settles and some anglers have fallen into them on their descent. Accessing the lakes where the bank slope is less severe is your best bet. Use a stick to prod through the snow for hidden crevasses.

During the open water seasons, both lakes can be fished from a boat; there are good boat launches on the Upper and Lower Lakes. You can also effectively fish the lakes from the shoreline. Trout, no matter what the species, love to cruise the shoreline when feeding. I have caught plenty of trout off of the shore on both lakes.

Kananaskis Lakes can be reached by traveling south on Highway 40, off of the Trans-Canada Highway. The lakes are approximately 136 km west of Calgary. It is a beautiful drive into the mountains. There are very good camping areas on both lakes, not far from the water but you may have to phone ahead for a reservation.

Above Photo: Anglers ice fishing the Lower Lake.
Below Photo: A typical lower Kananaskis rainbow trout.

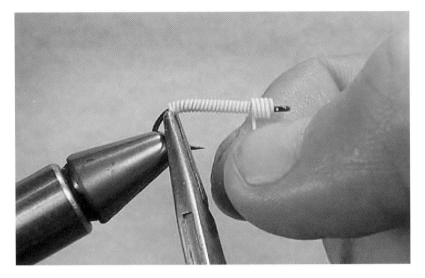

Part Ten
Making Your Own Lures

A major part of my fishing experience involves creating the lures that I fish with. It is very rewarding to catch a sport fish on something that you have designed and built from scratch. Outside of the hooks and materials that I use to tie jigs and flies, I can't remember that last time that I bought a lure from a store. Mind you, I still have a huge stock of tackle in the basement that is there if I need it.

Besides the gratification that I get from fishing with my home made lures, I find that I have also saved a lot of money over the years. Presently, it cost me any where from about 15 cents to around $1.50 to tie my own jigs and flies for fishing. I have accumulated a rather large stock of jig and fly tying materials over time; especially when I started commercial fly tying back in the late 1980's.

Another reason that I prefer to tie my own lures is that I can do so on single barb-less hooks. Most of my catch is live released and I find that treble hooks are too damaging on fish, small ones in particular. I know that this may tick off a few major lure manufacturers but until they catch on, it will be their loss. These days, I don't need to use treble hooks in my sport.

Many fishers are intimidated by the notion of having to learn how to tie a jig or a fly, but it is really very simple to do. You don't need a bunch of expensive equipment to get started. A fly tying vise, thread, bobbin, scissors and head cement are essential; the rest can be scrounged from around the house.

A friend of mine by the name of Mike Fenton, first showed me how to dub the thread, tie on a hackle and whip finish the head. This took place back in the early 1980's and for the first 3 years that I tie flies thereafter; I simply used half hitches to finish the head on my fly patterns. I know of a number of accomplished fly tiers that finish their fly's the same way.

If you plan on doing a lot of fly tying, you may want to take some instruction along the way, but for simple jigs and fly patterns I will review a few techniques and patterns that will help get you started. The savings that you gain after tying the first three dozen jigs or flies should pay for your initial investment.

Tying Equipment

As I mentioned, you will only need four basic pieces of equipment to get started. A fly tying vise is a must and can be purchased at a sporting goods store or fly fishing shop. You don't have to spend a lot of money, a simple cam vise will do. The second most important tool is you're tying thread and bobbin; this can also be purchase with the vise. The required scissors can be bought at a dollar store, nail clipper design are adequate. Clear finger nail polish will work for head cement or you can by the real stuff at a fly shop, when you buy your tying vise and other tools.

For tying your half hitches to complete the fly or jig pattern, a tip section of a ball point pen will do. Jigs hooks that have a round lead head require a tube, such as a plastic straw for tying a half hitch over the head. Hooks, jig heads and materials can be purchased at most sporting goods stores.

Wire Worms

The easiest jig to tie is the wire worm. This pattern is used primarily for fishing for Lake Whitefish during the winter months. The pattern is most effective when it is baited with a maggot or small piece of worm. It is tied by wrapping a small 28 gauge wire wrapping wire, around the shank of a standard or jig hook. The wire is purchased at most good electronic stores and comes in a variety of colors. My preference is yellow, olive, red, orange, black and copper.

You can tie this pattern by cutting an appropriate length of wire and wrap the hook shank from the bend of the hook forward to the eye of the hook, then wrap back over the head area with about four or five wraps. Try and keep the wire wraps as tight as possible as you tie the pattern. There is a picture of this process on the previous page. When you complete the wrapping, trim the ends of the wire and apply some head cement over the entire body, to help keep the pattern together when fishing it.

I use a pair of hemostat pliers locked onto the end of the wire when I start wrapping the pattern. This allows a good tight wrap along the hook shank.

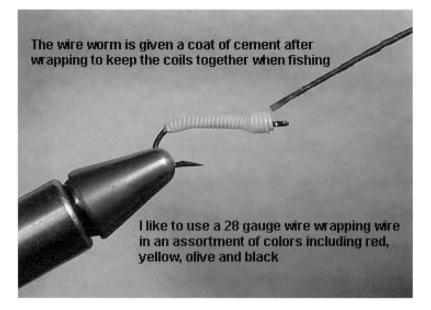

The wire worm is given a coat of cement after wrapping to keep the coils together when fishing

I like to use a 28 gauge wire wrapping wire in an assortment of colors including red, yellow, olive and black

If you know an electrician or a cable guy, your in luck, they can probably supply you with all you need in materials for this pattern. A popular version of this pattern is tied on a jig hook, so that the worm is fished horizontal while jigging. I have also tied this pattern on a standard hook with a monofilament jigging loop tied in on the underside of the hook shank.

The Standard Hook - Jigging Loop

I found that with the majority of small jig hooks that are available, the hook shanks are pretty weak and when you hook into a large fish while using them, they have a tendency to bend. It was with this problem in mind that I first decided to tie a jig using a standard heavy wire hook that is readily available in most stores that sell basic fishing equipment.

The challenge in tying a jig with a standard hook was in creating a strong enough loop near the mid-point of the hook shank, to attach my line to. My goal was to fish the jig pattern horizontally, with an effective action and still land a fish when I hooked one. I tried solving this challenge by tying in a monofilament loop at the front ¼ of the underside of a standard hook shank.

The monofilament loop is made from a small length of 10 .lb test. First I make a very small loop, using a perfection loop knot. I then cut the tag end of the loop about 2 cm down from the knot. I tie in the tag end near the eye of the hook and wrap thread over it back toward the bend, then double the loop back towards the eye and wrap it on forward with the thread. When you wrap the hook shank with a heavy lead wire, this helps keep the loop positioned perpendicular to the hook shank.

Tying Instructions

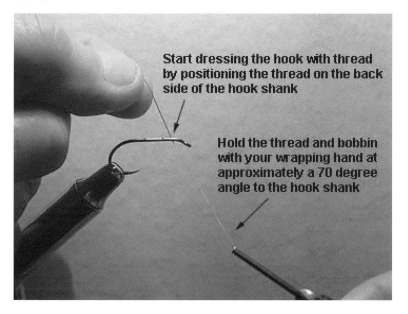

Start dressing the hook with thread by positioning the thread on the back side of the hook shank

Hold the thread and bobbin with your wrapping hand at approximately a 70 degree angle to the hook shank

The first step in tying a jig or fly is to dress the hook shank with thread.

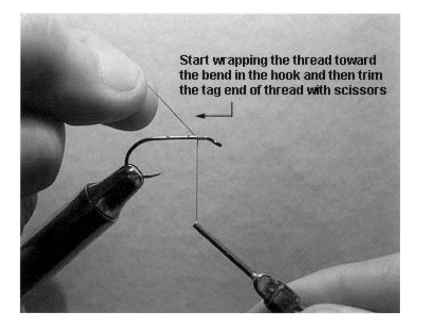

Start wrapping the thread toward the bend in the hook and then trim the tag end of thread with scissors

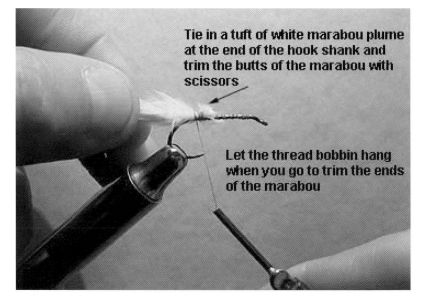

Tie in a tuft of white marabou plume at the end of the hook shank and trim the butts of the marabou with scissors

Let the thread bobbin hang when you go to trim the ends of the marabou

Marabou feather is commonly used for tying fishing jigs. On this pattern white is used.

Tie in a short length of 10.lb monofilament with a loop. Finish by wrapping the loop back towards the eye of the hook at the 3/4 point on the shank

Wrap the hook shank with 1 mm lead or solder wire for weight. The wire will help position the mono-loop at the right angle on the hook shank

The lead wire is coated with typewriter white-out so that it does not show through the white chenille when it is wet.

Wrap hook shank with 1.2 mm lead wire or solder

Paint the lead wire with typewriter white out

Tie a 10.lb monofilament loop to the shank of the hook. Tie on a length of white chennille

This is what the jig looks like when it is completed and ready to fish

The first day on the ice a few winters ago, I found out rather quickly that the jig pattern was a winner! I was fishing the Ghost Lake for lake trout and I had tied up a white marabou jig on a size 4 heavy wire bait hook. I topped the jig that morning with a small piece of smelt for a little added scent to the pattern.

I was fishing just off the shoreline in about 12 feet of water, in my little portable shack. I could clearly see my jig just off of the bottom, as I danced it up and down in subtle motion. I was very impressed with the jig pattern's swimming action as it darted about in a random movement. By positioning the mono-loop close to the middle of the hook shank, I was getting better action than a standard jig hook.

Suddenly, in a blink of an eye, a small lake trout appeared and consumed the small white jig. I set the hook and had him on. I had been concerned about the mono-loops close proximity to the point of the hook and whether it would affect my ability to set the hook successfully. Now I knew that this was not an issue.

After a few chuckles, I pulled the small laker up out of the ice, removed the jig and released the fish back into the lake. Since that time I have caught a number of lake trout on this pattern and it has become one of my favorites for fishing shallower areas on lakes and reservoirs. It even works great for rainbow and brown trout, when topped with a small piece of worm.

With the limited amount of led wire that can be applied, the jig is effective in depths of up to 15 feet. After that, the jig does not respond to your jigging with light test line. I have also fished this pattern with success, stationary, just off of the bottom as a still bait.

Wire Worms

Little Rocket Jigs

Pike and Lake Trout Jigs

Home Made Flies
and Jigs

Standard Hook Jigs

Mag Flies

Trophy Trout
Trolling Flies

Little Rocket Jigs

With this jig pattern being tied on a standard jig hook in well known colors, I'm confident that some one at some time has probably tied this pattern before. I first designed the jig pattern for ice fishing the Upper Kananaskis Lake for rainbow trout. The idea behind my choice of color for the jig was to use colors that were powerful attractants. Once the trout noticed the florescent colors it would come in for a closer look and take the offering of bait on the hook.

I use one specific type of bait when ice fishing this jig. A small ½" piece of worm is cut from a full body dew worm or large garden variety. The worm is thread onto the hook in a parallel fashion. The jig is also actually fished stationary, suspended off of the bottom in deep water or about a foot off of the bottom in shallower water.

The weight of the lead wrapped body is all that is necessary to get the jig down to the right depth. I then hook a bobber onto the line and rest the bobber on the edge of the augured hole. On colder days when the hole is icing up, I take a short flat piece of lath and put it over the hole, balancing the bobber on the wood at the centre of the hole. When the bobber is pulled into the hole you can dash over and watch for when the bobber is pulled under, at this point in time you can quickly set the hook.

If there are large trout present in the lake or reservoir, I use a standard hook with a jig loop of monofilament in the pattern. The basic jig hook pattern is faster to tie but there are situations where bending a hook and loosing a trout can be very frustrating. I like to tie this pattern on a size 8 or size 6 heavy wire hook.

Since I started using this Little Rocket Jig for ice fishing, it has produced great results on stocked rainbow trout. It is almost always my first choice of tackle when the holes are augured. I have theory that because the weight on the jig is hidden beneath a cover of chenille, the trout do not feel anything hard when they first touch the jig; the bait does the rest.

Mag Flies

The Mag Fly pattern was designed for catching whitefish through the ice. The name came from the patterns use with a Maggot for bait. I designed this pattern back in the 1980's for fishing the Ghost Lake and it has become a popular fly pattern, not only for me but for a number of ice fishers ever since. I've sold 100's of this pattern in the Cochrane area over the years.

The first Mag fly that I tied consisted of a small piece of fluorescent chenille, with a few wraps of hackle feather at the head of the hook shank. The idea was much the same as the Little Rocket Jig, the bright colors would attract the fish in and the maggot bait would do the rest. In the early 1990's I added a wrap of tinsel to the body of the fly to compliment its appearance and help attract fish.

I tie this pattern on a size 12 to 16 heavy wire short shank hook, such as a Mustad 3906 or 3906B. For the past few years, I have been tying in a looped 6 .lb test leader onto the hook shank. This is a bonus when your ice fishing and your fingers are cold, you can use a loop to loop connection to set up your line. In the following tying instructions, I will leave this part out, to make it easier for you to learn the basic pattern.

I prefer to fish this fly in the shallower water near the shoreline of a lake in 4 to 20 feet of water. You can set up two flies spaced about one foot apart, with the sinker on the bottom or you can fish one pattern with a small split shot one foot up, if you are fishing suspended above the bottom. In either case, I like to use a small bobber set on the edge of the ice or on a piece of wood lath over the hole.

When you fish two flies on a line, the extra fly will give you more time to set the hook on a hungry fish. If the trout or whitefish takes your bait on one fly, they will usually start on the second fly as you are running to your hole.

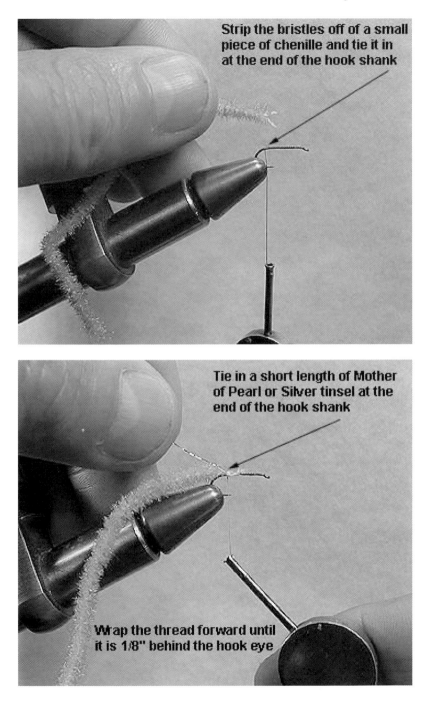

Strip the bristles off of a small piece of chenille and tie it in at the end of the hook shank

Tie in a short length of Mother of Pearl or Silver tinsel at the end of the hook shank

Wrap the thread forward until it is 1/8" behind the hook eye

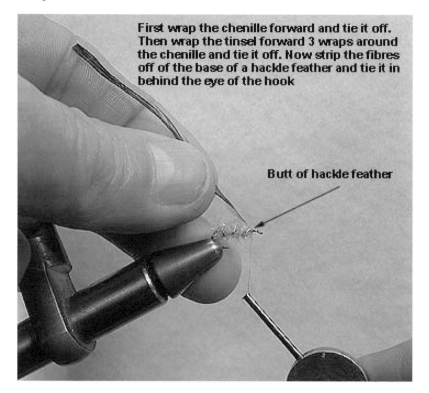

First wrap the chenille forward and tie it off. Then wrap the tinsel forward 3 wraps around the chenille and tie it off. Now strip the fibres off of the base of a hackle feather and tie it in behind the eye of the hook

Butt of hackle feather

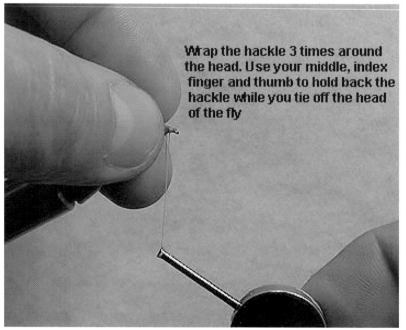

Wrap the hackle 3 times around the head. Use your middle, index finger and thumb to hold back the hackle while you tie off the head of the fly

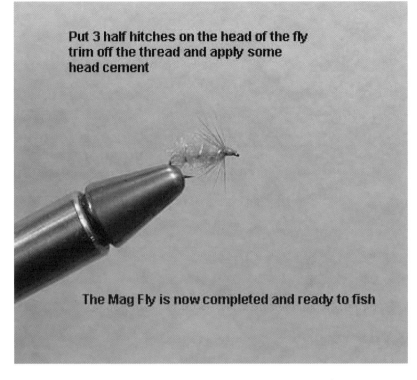

Put 3 half hitches on the head of the fly trim off the thread and apply some head cement

The Mag Fly is now completed and ready to fish

I have covered some very basic and easy to tie lures for you to get started. If you manage to learn to tie these patterns effectively, you will be ready to move on to some more difficult and complex jigs and flies, it is up to you!

Hooks and materials for tying your own lures can be purchased at some sporting goods stores and all fly shops. If you are in need of help when you walk thru the doors, don't be shy about asking for assistance. These people are accustom to dealing with beginners and they are generally eager to help get you started. It is also a great place to learn more about further options for your hobby.

The chenille that I use on all of my smaller jigs and mag flies is a small Trilobal Antron in a variety of colors. The most heavily used colors are white, hot pink, chartreuse and orange. For the mag flies, I also have good success tying them in olive green, dark green and brown. I like to use a red 6/0 thread for tying most small jigs and mag flies. Does it make a difference? I don't know; but why mess with success!

I'm confident that after you catch your first fish on one of your own lures you will be hooked. Another benefit to this facet of your sport is that you can experiment with different designs targeting different lakes, reservoirs and species of fish in your area.

Percy and Marjorie Copithorne with fish from the Jumpingpound Creek, Alberta – 1904-05

Part Eleven

The Jumpingpound Creek Strain

From its source at the base of Jumpingpound Mountain, in the Fisher Range of mountains, the Jumpingpound Creek flows along the Powder Face trail down through a high mountain valley into the foothills just west of the City of Calgary. The creek is approximately 80 km in length from the mountain that bares its name to where it enters the Bow River in the Town of Cochrane.

For the last 30 or so kilometers, the stream passes through cattle ranch country with open grasslands and rolling hills. The creek is sheltered by its defined valley bottom with plenty of riparian cover to shade its waters and the trout that live there. As a young fellow, I spent many an hour trying to catch a few trout for my creel along the banks of this part of the Jumping-pound's reach. Up until the early 1960's, when the province stopped stocking the stream with trout, the creek was a popular destination for many trout anglers.

Prior to the introduction of rainbow trout in the 1930's, the Jumping-pound held a population of native cutthroat trout. As a result of this combination of species, the blood lines are mixed and on many of the trout, you can visually see the influences of this cross breeding, some anglers call them "cutt-bows". However, predominantly, most of the trout are closer to a true rainbow trout. Today, on the upper reaches of the creek, you can still find cutthroat trout, many of which have been planted there in recent years.

After the stocking program ended early 60's, the absences of hatchery trout lead to a decline in the streams popularity with many anglers. This didn't mean that the trout fishing on the stream ended, it is just that the rainbow trout that were present in the JP from that point of time on, were wild fish and not as easy to catch. Back in those days, fishing was all about catching a limit for the creel and dinner table, very little thought was directed at conservation and sustainability.

Over the years, since the creek's glory days as a popular trout stream, the JP carried its reputation amongst long time anglers as the trout stream that "use to be". Little did we realize at that time that the streams importance to the areas trout fishery was being over looked! There were always plenty of small trout present in the stream and those that were fishing to catch trout to eat, found this a little annoying. These small trout would aggressively take just about anything that they could get their mouths around.

It wasn't until years later that the Jumpingpound Creek was identified as the only key tributary, between the Ghost and Bearspaw dams that rainbow trout used to spawn in. The JP was actually more important as a recruitment and nursery stream. Rainbow trout would lay their eggs, while spawning in the stream and after the trout hatched, they would spend the first year or so in the creek, before they moved downstream into the Bow River. This is why it is called a nursery stream.

Starting in the 1970's, a drought cycle started to impact the Bow River watershed, flow conditions on all of the area streams started to diminish. Warmer water conditions affected the survival rate of trout and these influences were felt by trout anglers on all of their favorite area flowing waters. The Jumpingpound was especially hit hard. Some area ranchers started to notice fish kills on the creek, something that they could not recall happening in the past.

These turbulent times started a movement in trout fishing circles. When you witness dramatic change in something that you love so much, you begin to question why and many are compelled to take action. A change in fisheries management was needed. No longer could our trout waters sustain the generous harvest limits that were allowed and changes were bound to be made. The words "Conservation, Protection and Enhancement" became part of the fishing conversation amongst committed anglers.

The first step in management change was an important one! The reduction of allowable harvest limits - which would evolve over time. This made prefect sense! When the flow in a trout stream is lower than normal for a number of years, trout have a tendency to stack up in the deeper pools where the water is cooler in the depths and the trout are sheltered by the available habitat. When the trout season opens, there is a rush to be first on the water, to fish these pools and the numerous trout that are present.

As the trout season progresses, the numbers of trout available decline in number, along with the catches and inevitable harvests of trout. In this scenario, those that are first, have good recreation and bounty and those that follow - do not. It is not what you would call a "conservation minded" perspective but you have to bear in mind that most anglers, at the time, were totally oblivious of their impacts to the long term viability of their resource. It was considered an excepted practice, back in the old days. Your status as an angler was measured by your harvest of trout.

As far as I can remember, there has always been a spring closure on the Jumpingpound Creek, to protect the rainbow and cutthroat trout that spawn there in the spring. However, there was never any kind of study conducted to confirm this fact. Up until 1996, there was no protection for the mature trout that staged in the Bow River near the mouth of the JP, prior to their accent up the creek to spawn, in the spring. During this early season event, many anglers would be free to harvest these larger trout in the Bow River when they were the most vulnerable in April and May every year.

The fact that large rainbow trout were being harvested every spring, prior to moving up into the JP Creek, was a well kept secret for a few area anglers. For those anglers that recognized the importance of these huge pre-spawn rainbows, it was frustrating to know that the fish were getting hammered and the result would be less trout in the system in future years. Something had to be done. However, without a study competed to confirm that the fishery was being impacted by harvest; most complaints to the regional biologists were going nowhere. It would take a major grassroots effort to get things rolling. This opportunity came about in 1992.

Daryl Downs, President of the recently formed "Jumpingpound Chapter of Trout Unlimited" identified a problem near the mouth of the JP Creek and the Bow River in the early spring of 1992. For years there was a small fork in the JP just upstream of the confluence and in 1990, beavers had moved in and built some huge dams across the channel creating a major obstacle for migrating trout. In the winter of 91 and 92, most of the streams flow had been diverted into this small side channel by ice dams on the creek.

With the side channels flow entering the Bow River downstream of the old creek mouth, that was pretty much dry that spring, the rainbow trout were forced to travel up this new route to get to their spawning grounds. With the huge dams present and little hope of high flows from spring runoff that year, something had to be done.

Daryl called me on the phone and explained the situation, so we arranged a meeting at the creek to look things over. Sure enough, there were hundreds of very large rainbow trout trapped below the large beaver dams on the side channel. Daryl explained that the chapter membership were eager to move on this situation if a plan was in place. I had experience with permitting for in-stream fish habitat enhancement work on the JP Creek before, so I offered to help out, with organizing a plan and getting the necessary permits to do something about this situation. The fact that it was an emergency and the seasons spawning success on the creek was at stake, would help in rushing thru the permitting part of the projects objective.

The following week, all of the permits required were in place and a contractor with a track hoe arrived on site. The plan was to excavate down into the old stream channel directly below the fork in the creek and dam off the new side channel with the spoil. In the mean time, volunteers from the local JP Chapter of TU and the Cochrane Scouts and ventures would assist in the beaver dam removal and rescue the trapped trout to be moved back into the Bow River, where they could travel up the old creek channel after the project was completed. Nets of all shapes and sizes were used to gather the trapped trout and put them in five gallon buckets for their short trip to the Bow River.

Above Photo: The Cochrane Ventures and Scouts helped out with the beaver dam removal and the trout rescue program.

By the late afternoon that day, the project was completed, all of the trapped trout were removed from the side channel and the new riffle created in the old creek bed was looking very good. The next day, I traveled the shoreline of the Bow River for approximately 2 km downstream to see if there were any dead trout. There wasn't. That evening I called a few volunteers on the phone to see if they could join me for a similar survey up the Jumpingpound Creek on the following day.

The following morning I met two volunteers at the bridge across the JP Creek in Bow Meadows. It was a warm spring morning promising blue skies

Above Photo: This is what the old JP Creek channel looked like before the project was completed.

Below Photo: This is the same area of channel after the new channel work was completed.

for the day, a good day for a walk on the creek. We traveled about two kilometers up the creek before we encountered our first trout. It was a pair of large rainbow trout spawning near the banks in about 10 inches of water.

From that point on, we started seeing lots of spawning trout. Because of their large size and their dark coloration, they were easy to spot. After traveling 4 km upstream, we found only one dead trout, a rainbow of about 23 inches in length. We didn't know whether it had died as a result of the stress in the trout rescue or of natural causes, it was the only dead fish that we found.

That evening, I phoned the owner of the land on which we saw the spawning trout and obtained permission to return there the next day to video some of the spawning activity. I thought that this footage would be useful if it was passed on to the right provincial biologist. Having seen this spawning activity on the creek in previous years, while monitoring a fish habitat enhancement project that I had completed in 1987, it was time to capture the event on camera.

The next day, I drove my truck down into the valley bottom on an access trail and parked above a high steep bank to see if the trout were still spawning in the area below. They were! From that vantage point, I was able to sneak down the bank to a location just above two pair of spawning trout that were about 18 to 20 inches in length. After filming those trout, I moved downstream and found plenty of spawning trout to capture on film. I managed to get some great footage that day and returned home with about one hour on my video tape.

A few days following my survey of the spawning activity on the creek, I called Roger Packham, a provincial fisheries biologist for the area. I explained that I had some good video verifying the use of the lower end of Jumpingpound Creek as a rainbow trout spawning habitat. I asked him if he would be interested in viewing the footage at my home and when a meeting would be convenient for him.

I had worked with Roger on a few projects in the past and I liked his enthusiasm regarding fisheries related issues in the Cochrane area. As expected, Roger was very interested in seeing some hard evidence that rainbow trout were using the JP Creek as a spawning area. I had previously mentioned to him that the spring migrating rainbow trout were getting hit pretty hard on the Bow River, prior to moving up the creek to spawn and this was my chance to gain his support in doing something about the situation.

During the spring, a few years earlier, I had helped Roger remove some beaver dams on the lower end of the Jumpingpound to allow any spawning trout an easy passage up the creek. The day of that outing, I was disappointed that we hadn't seen any trout below the dams at that time. It was possible that most of the trout that year were trapped below the dams on the side channel near the mouth.

A week after I had contacted Roger, he had been in Cochrane on some other business, so he arranged to meet me to view the video that I had promised to show him. He was very impressed with not only the number of rainbow trout that were spawning but also the size of these fish. I could tell from his enthusiasm that he was ready to move on some kind of study program to further establish this run of trout on the creek.

At that point in time, I explained to Roger that the local chapter of Trout Unlimited would probably be eager and willing to help get something started on this matter. After the success of the channel project near the mouth of the JP that spring, I knew that there was definitely enough interest and the club had a good executive to motivate the membership.

Roger suggested preparing a proposal to conduct a spawning survey on the JP in the spring of the year. Constructing a fence and trap on the creek's lower end to capture migrating trout and tagging them after their weight and length was recorded. This would establish the Jumpingpound Creek's importance as a spawning tributary and also provide an opportunity to track the rainbow trout's movements after the spawning season. I agreed to help out and committed to contact the TU Chapters president to run the idea by him. We could arrange a meeting with the club's executive and Roger for a later date.

The proposal idea was accepted with enthusiasm by the TU members. It was decided that Ed Johnson and Daryl Downs would prepare a proposal document and seek funding opportunities from the Alberta Conservation Association for the program. Roger also agreed to help secure a consultant to handle the trapping equipment, the expertise and the final report and analysis. The following spring of 1993 was the target date for getting this project organized and in place.

As April of 1993 approached, there was growing excitement amongst the club membership. The success of the channel project the year before had ignited interest in the clubs namesake; the"Jumpingpound Chapter" and the run of trout that depend on the creek for their survival. I had been voted into the club as Habitat Chairman and now I had the responsibility that goes along with the title. The plan was that I would monitor the creek channel to let the consultant know when the ice left the banks enough that the trap and fence could be installed in the creek.

During a tour of the creek in early April, Roger Packham, Paul Hvenegaard of D.A. Westworth & Associates and I picked a spot on the creek for the trapping site. It was located approximately 1.5 km upstream of the confluence with the Bow River. Permission was obtained from the landowners for access and a work station. It was a pretty spot hidden in a tall stand of cottonwood and spruce trees where the creek flowed along a steep tree covered bank on the far side of the channel.

On April 16th, the consultant staff met with the club volunteers on the chosen site to install the fish trap and fence. It was a cool morning with the smells of spring thaw in the air. The water was extremely cold and flowing relatively clear. The bank ice at the site was still intact and would have to be removed for the fence on both sides of the channel. It was going to be hard work but there were about 12 sets of hands on site and a lot of enthusiasm.

The trap fence was designed to direct migrating trout into the main box trap in the centre of the channel. This was accomplished by having the wings of the fence on the upstream and downstream side of the trap, installed in a funnel shape across the channel. When a trout encountered the fence, it would follow it in the direction it was swimming until it entered the conical

Above Photo: This is a photo of the trout trap taken from the high banks above the JP Creek.

entrance hole in the trap. Much the same as a minnow trap, if you're familiar with such a contraption.

Twice a day, in the early morning and again in the afternoon, the trap was tended. Any trout captured were processed on the shoreline. First the fish were anesthetized (put under) and then they were measured, weighed and a small visual implant tag with a number was injected into a membrane just behind the fish's eye.

The idea behind the numbered tag, was that if the same trout was caught somewhere on the river system later on in the season, the number could be recorded and we would know how far and where the trout had traveled. After the trap was set, we all parted ways and a plan to tend the trap was scheduled to start the next morning on the creek.

That next morning we were surprised to find that there were six rather large trout in our trap. This was great news, because now we knew that these trout start moving up the JP Creek as soon as the ice is off of the stream channel. The big question was; how many trout had already traveled up the creek before the trap was in? In any case, the project was off the ground and we were now in business and underway with the study.

Everyday, for the rest of the month of April, we had trout in our trap! We were processing around 8 fish a day. Considering the time of the year, things could get only better. Rainbow trout will not spawn until the water temperatures get up to approximately 10 degrees Celsius and the water temperatures were still down in the 6 to 8 degree range. As time progressed and the creek started to warm up, more trout were bound to follow.

In our last week of April, we encountered our first problem in the trapping program. Some type of animal was chewing up the plastic mesh used for the trap's construction. The consultant was quick to replace the material on the trap with expanded metal but we needed to do something else to keep the hungry fish feeders from dinning on our trout. I came up with the idea of a scare crow to watch over the trap when nobody was around. It sounds kind of silly but something so simple might keep predators from causing us some major grief.

A scare crow ("Jake") was built out of some old cloths and a hat and placed in a sitting position on the top of the trap cage. It worked great; we didn't have any problems for the next few weeks! That was until our furry fisher friend discovered that Jake was just a big dummy. One morning we found some fish bones and parts on the top of the entrance cone to the trap, on the inside. It was time to take care of our night time visitor!

I contacted the local Fish and Wildlife officer, Stan Hawes and asked if he had a spare live trap available for our problem. He said he did and that we could use it for a while. The trap was mainly used for trapping skunks and it had a familiar odor to it when I picked it up the following day. After a thorough scrubbing and deodorizing, the trap was ready for the site.

The night visitor left a few clues to his feeding habitats each morning when we arrived at the trap site. It appeared that he liked to enter the trap through the entrance cone, grab a trout and then sit on top of the entrance cone, which was flat, to dine on the trout. I thought that placing the live trap on the entrance cone would be the best placement for the trap. What ever it was that was eating our fish was bound to be curious and having the trap in an area that he had become familiar with, might be the best line of approach to capturing the varmint.

I didn't think that any type of bait was necessary in the trapping process. I thought that the culprit liked a fresh catch and like all fishermen, it also enjoyed the hunt for trout. It worked! The next morning we had captured an adult mink. It was fairly upset with its detainment and the mink let us know just that when the live trap was removed from the trout trap with its contents. I have never heard an angry threatened mink before but believe me they make a scary noise when they are captured live.

Now what to do? There was no way that we were going to harm the critter and if it was a female, there was a good chance that it had kittens nearby. The only thing that I could think of was to hold the mink captive for a day, to let the animal have plenty of time to realize it's mistake for eating our fish and just to let it sink in that given a second chance, it would go else where to dine.

We held the mink captive until the next day. Children that visited the site with their parents got a big kick out of the guilty inmate. That following afternoon, it was time to free the mink. One of the volunteers took the trapped animal just upstream of the trap site and opened the cage door. The mink wasted little time in heading for the cover of brush just upstream.

Above Photo: This is a photo of our captive inmate just before its release from the live trap.

This method of educating the mink worked great and the trap site was safe from predation for the following weeks.

The only other encounter with a fur bearing animal was a very large beaver that got trapped in with the trout one afternoon. We netted the beaver and moved it away from the site, alive and well. The beaver was about 40 or so pounds and darn near bent the net handle in the process.

In the first week of May the main run of rainbow trout started to move up the Jumpingpound Creek. We went from daily catch rates of approximately 8 to 10 trout, up to 30 plus trout per day by the end of the week. It was very satisfying to suddenly see so many fish in our traps every morning. They were all beautiful trout in perfect condition. None of them had the deformed mouths so typical on lower Bow River trout.

When you're handling so many rainbow trout in such a brief period of time, you're bound to see something interesting. Such was the case one day in mid May. A rainbow trout of about 18 inches in length was captured and when it was laid on the weigh scale, we noticed the bend of a hook sticking out of its "you know what"! Using my fingers, I grabbed the hook and pulled it out. What followed was a size 4 Doc Sprately fly pattern, still intact.

The trout must have swallowed the fly and broke off the leader. The hook had migrated thru the entire digestive system of the fish and by the ease with which it came out, it would have been passed in a few days anyway. The fishes vent around the hook was all swollen and enlarged. It is amazing that the trout had lived through the entire episode and it was still healthy and relatively in good shape.

As the later part of May bourgeoned with the new season's growth along the creek, our visitors to the site increased. This entire program was important from an educational perspective and having the opportunity to show some of the residents of Cochrane what was going on and how important the stream was in the natural scheme of things, was a bonus. We had friends of friends, school students and fellow anglers show up and some chipped in to help out.

Above Photo: This group of local kids helped out by netting some trout that got trapped between the wings of the fence.

The hot coffee was always in the pot and in the cool evenings a wood fire was there to warm up the bones, especially the fingers after tending the trap for the day. People were amazed at how many trout were being captured everyday. From the shoreline, you could climb along the fence out to where the trout were swimming in the trap for a look, without getting your feet wet. We would celebrate just about anything that made a record catch. The first 500 trout processed was celebrated, the first 1000 disserved a bonfire and a toast to our success.

The entire project went very smoothly and thanks to some key individuals the job was done in an efficient manor. These volunteers spent many hours of their free time to chip in. Pete Landry, Doc, Daryl Downs, Sandra Foss, Jack Bruce, Marshal Bye, Turk Graham, Andy Macri and the list goes on. All of these people had a keen interest in not only the Jumpingpound rainbow trout but also in the environment in which they live. The landowners and their neighbors joined in on our celebrations by the stream. It was a real community event.

By the first week of June, the trout trapping program on Jumpingpound Creek was completed. A total of 1,126 rainbow trout had been captured and processed during the spring trapping program. The entire project was a success and now all we had to do is wait until the report had been completed, before the benefits of this study could be fully realized. At least that is what we expected would happen! Unfortunately for us, our good friend Roger Packham, who had been instrumental in getting this project off the ground, had left his position with Fish and Wildlife.

Despite the Jumpingpound Chapter's efforts and hard work, there was no immediate change in the fishing regulations to protect the spring rainbow trout in the Bow River, just prior to their migration up the creek. The publicity from the trapping study had spread the word about the large trout that gathered to move up the JP to spawn. This attracted many anglers in the spring of 1994 and 1995; lots of trout were getting caught and killed over those two years. It was very disappointing for those of us that had thought that the study would result in special regulation changes to protect these trout, immediately after it had been completed.

After the spring of 1995, I was feed up with the situation. I was still habitat chairman of the JP Chapter, so I thought that hold that position might help me in a campaign to see some changes; but I knew that I would need some other help. I still had some contacts with the Sarcee and Calgary Fish and Game Association. I had worked with the Sarcee on a couple of projects in the past and I knew that I could count on them to support us, especially Bryce Chase. There was also the Alberta counsel of TU and the Bow River Chapter to contact.

I drafted a letter stating our cause and resolution, forwarding it with another letter of request for support, to all the clubs and organizations that I knew. We had a good case and we had just completed a very worthwhile study that would help us out with our goal. The fact that the existing regulations allowed for a 5 fish harvest of these beautiful rainbow trout was the determining factor that I was confident would win us support.

When March 1st of 1996 came, I was a regular visitor to the Cochrane Fish & Wildlife office. At that time, as usual, the regulation booklet was late coming in, so I had to make a few trips before I got my copy. Finally, the regulation book arrived; it sat on the passenger seat of my truck for the drive home. I was anxious but also ready for disappointment. This is something that you have to prepare yourself for, it seems, when you are relying on fisheries managers to make the right decision.

After thumbing through the pages at my kitchen table, I came to the fisheries management zone in our area. There – under the Jumpingpound and Bow River regulations - was what I wanted to see. It was like Christmas; we had our regulation change! Effective that spring, there was a "O" harvest limit on rainbow trout, from the mouth of the JP Creek downstream to a specified point on the Bow River.

It is interesting to note that in 1998, sweeping regulation changes came about for the entire province of Alberta. In those new regulations, the entire Bow River between Ghost and Bearspaw Dams received a spring "No Harvest of Trout" regulation to protect the rainbow trout in the system. These province wide regulation changes were made as a result of provincial open house meetings that were held by fisheries managers to determine the direction in which fisheries management should go. Anglers like you and me, as stake holders, had a say in the matter!

Above Photo: This was one of the few cut-bow hybrids that we captured in our trap. Note the heavy dark spots above the lateral line.
Below Photo: This is a typical JP strain of rainbow trout.

Glenbow Archives NA-4312-49

Above Photo: Ranch visitor fishing, Bow River Ranch, Cochrane area, Alberta. – 1926. (Authors Note): I believe that this photo was taken just downstream of the present day River Avenue Bridge, in Cochrane.

Part Twelve
The Bow River

Plenty has been written about the lower Bow River, meaning the reach of river below the Bearspaw Dam that flows to the east and south of Calgary. How you define a particular stretch of the Bow is dependant on where you live. From my perspective, upstream of the Bearspaw Dam to the Ghost Reservoir is what I would call the middle Bow River and from there to its headwaters flows the upper Bow River.

Both the middle Bow and the upper reach are not as famous as the lower Bow, which has earned its reputation from the consistently good trout fishing and also the size of trout that can be caught there. The upper Bow River, downstream of Bow Falls in Banff Park, is full of brown trout and mountain whitefish and on certain days can produce great fishing. However, these brown trout are not easy trout to catch by nature and some days they are very particular about what they will feed on.

The brown trout are immigrants to North America, not native trout. They are respected and revered by anglers as a difficult trout to catch. It could be that the centuries of being angled for in both Europe and Britain have made these trout that way, through natural selection. The story is that a hatchery truck with a load of brown trout broke down on the road near Carrot Creek in Banff, back in the 1920's, so the driver dumped the load of fish into the creek or the nearby river, rather than let them die.

The brown trout has adapted well to its new environment and populates the river system in large numbers. I have fished the upper Bow for years and I enjoy not only the trout fishing but also the beautiful scenery that comes with it. There are small pockets of brook trout along the upper Bow Rivers course that will also provide some great angling.

The upper Bow River, like the middle Bow is impacted by fluctuating water levels created by power generation facilities from watershed dams. This has an influence on the quality of fishing on both reaches of river. It is important that you know this little bit of information, if you're wading on the upper Bow. In some areas there are numerous side channels that you can wade across when the flows are low, during non-peak demand for electricity. Then, all of a sudden, the water levels can come up and you're stranded on an island.

One of the primary bonuses of fishing the upper Bow is the ease of access. The old 1-A highway travels along one side of the river, with the Trans Canada highway on the other. There are plenty of good parking spots to get close to the river. In recent years, Alberta Transportation has constructed a large fence along the Trans Canada to keep wildlife off of the highway; this has disrupted access for many of the regulars that fish the upper Bow.

The middle Bow River is familiar home water for me. Over the years, as a boy, adolescent and as an adult, I have fished every foot of this reach of river from the Bearspaw to the Ghost. I refer to this length of the river as the "Not so Famous" Bow River. The water levels fluctuate from high flows to extremely low flows daily during certain seasons of the year.

For example; as I write this line, yesterday the volume of flow coming out of the Ghost Dam Power Plant dropped from 168.5 CMS, at 4:00 P.M. in the afternoon, to 9.5 CMS at 10:00 P.M. in the evening. The impacts of these extreme variances in flow are just too harsh on the fish populations downstream. It affects their food supply and disrupts their habitat in which they live. This is why the fishing along this reach of the Bow River has never been able to reach its full potential. However, there is still a fishery in these waters!

The fish in this stretch of water have learned to be highly mobile in their attempts to survive. During the early spring and late summer months, the trout and whitefish learn to move from one (low water) habitat, to another entirely different (high water) habitat, on a daily basis. It is now late November and most of the rivers populations of fish have moved downstream into the Bearspaw Reservoir to spend the winter months.

The remaining fish will spend their winter months trying to seek out a living in some of the deeper wintering pools along the river. Prior to the new fishing regulations, I have fished the Bow River between the dams on Chinook days over the winter months and caught both trout and whitefish. The fish that I have caught in the late winter are usually fairly thin and not in good form.

With all of this information, you would think that the fishery along this length is not worth while! This is not so! I have fished the Bow around the Town of Cochrane for many years and I have had some great recreation. The river's fishery can be influenced by bad winters and run-off events on the only spawning tributary which is the Jumpingpound Creek, but there are always fish to be caught.

There is also a lot of potential to improve the fishery on the river in future years. Tributaries like the Bighill Creek and Grand Valley Creek have a huge amount of potential if they are cleaned up and brought back to an acceptable level of health. To accomplish this, we need to focus on the existing agricultural activities that are presently being used on the watershed.

Both of these creeks were once prime fishing destinations for trout anglers. Over the years, the two streams have degraded to the point where it will take some time for the results of any efforts to bring them back, to be noticed. I am confident that this will happen eventually, the sooner the better. When it does happen, we will have two more spawning tributaries to the Bow, besides only one (JP Creek).

Back in the 1960's and 70's, I would travel the banks of the Bow and cast for trout and whitefish, with a creel on my waist, kept cool with water from the river. I must confess that at the time, I wasn't overly concerned with the modern day conservation consciousness that I should have had. In any case, I would usually return home with a nice catch of both trout and whitefish for the pan.

The average size trout would be around 12 to 14 inches, probably three year old fish. They were what we called back then, "pan size". In the process of catching a few for the creel, I would always catch numerous small trout, ranging in size from about 4 to 8 inches. Every now and then, a monster of 16 to 18 inches took my offering. This was rare on most of the river's length, except for in the spring months.

I didn't know why at the time, but in the spring, some very large trout moved into the system. These larger trout were most likely from the

Bearspaw Dam further downstream, I thought. Over time, I began to pin point where the largest trout were to be had and at what time of year. Eventually the puzzle started to take shape. The more numerous large trout could be caught near the confluence of the Jumpingpound Creek in the spring of the year.

Years earlier, I had fished the Bow River near the mouth of the JP with an old timer and well known local fisherman, Harry Hart. I remember him pointing out the large trout holding in the pools below the steep clay bank on the north side of the river, across from the JP. At that time I didn't really think about why they were there in such great numbers but rather, I concentrated on how I was going to catch them.

If ever there was a fisherman's secret worth keeping, this was it! Fishing for these large pre-spawn rainbow trout was my own little piece of heaven. Further downstream, below the Highway 22 bridge, every spring, anglers would show up to fish for the large trout that were present in the bridge pool. However, I doubt that they knew why the trout were there at that time of the year. I think that they just knew that there was great fishing to be had on the Bow River in the spring months.

Over time, I evolved into a more conservation minded individual and my impact on the area fishery was less of an issue for my conscious. What ever the case, I felt that I should help protect and conserve the fishery resource that I had taken so much from and enjoyed over the years. It wouldn't hurt to put a little something back for future generations!

In the mid 1980's there was a growing movement in fisheries circles that helped generate some major changes in the protection of fish habitat and the management of fish populations in our streams and lakes. There were also a few individuals that were taking measures to create fish habitat on waters that had been negatively impacted by the activities of humans. I started developing a major interest in the later.

My first contact with members of this group came about when I was introduced to Bill Griffiths and Al Sosiak, both of whom were provincial fisheries biologists in the Calgary area. When I explained my interest in some local fisheries issues to both gentlemen, they were very eager to help out, if I was prepared to do something about it. That is when it all started for me; I had made a commitment to try and help make some positive changes in the fishery that had been so good to me over the years.

There were two main goals that I had given careful thought about for some time. The first was the protection of the Bow River strain of rainbow trout between the Ghost and Bearspaw Dams, primary the spring spawning run of rainbow trout that moves up the JP Creek to spawn in the spring. The second goal was related to the very large fluctuations in the river's water levels over a 24 hour time period, each day. Both of these were pretty daunting issues but they both had major influence over the fishery on this reach of the Bow River.

I knew that my chances of getting changes in the daily flow conditions on the river would be pointless, so I thought why not concentrate on the creation of low water flow habitat for trout. This approach is something that would be possible and with the growing movement in that direction in other watersheds, well within the realm of achievement.

At the time I thought that the protection of the spawning run of rainbow trout should not be a major challenge, considering my argument. However, this was going to turn out to be a major hurtle over the coming years, as I would find out later on. A regulation change to protect the trout would require the input of the provincial fisheries biologists that represent that area of the province, so I began my campaign by letting them know of the situation.

The fish habitat enhancement idea on the Bow River would also require their input and help to accomplish. I was rather lucky, at the time, to be dealing with biologist Bill Griffiths. After running an idea of creating some boulder habitat on the river to provide low flow cover for trout, he was immediately interested. With the river having immense volumes of flow in the spring run-off and severe ice conditions throughout some winters, large boulders was what I thought would be the best choice of habitat enhancement for the system.

In 1986, Bill recruited River Engineer, Sheldon Lowe, of Alberta Environments, River Engineering Branch, for some consulting for the project and we arranged a meeting on the river to discuss some ideas. When the meeting took place, Sheldon agreed to draw up a plan for some enhancement work at the River Avenue Bridge area on the Bow River in Cochrane. Sheldon Lowe would later go on to publish the guidelines manual "Fish Habitat Enhancement Designs – Typical Structures". The manual has since become an integral reference for me and other people in the field.

I agreed to take care of the fund raising efforts and hiring the contractor to complete the project. This was going to be an experimental pilot project, so the scale was relatively small for a big river like the Bow, but that was to be expected for such an idea. Winter ice conditions carry a tremendous amount of force and we had to be sure that not only the size of the boulders was adequate but also their placement in the river channel had to be correct.

I was just excited that I actually had an opportunity to participate in such a project! This could open the door for future improvements in the river's fish habitat and benefit the trout that would utilize the newly created environment. At that particular site, when the water levels in the river go down over night and into the early morning hours, trout are forced to move a considerable distance downstream, to deeper water. Once our enhancement work is completed, the trout will be able to move from a shoreline habitat along the banks, to a low water habitat just metres out from the bank during low flows.

Over the winter of 1986-87, Sheldon completed a design for the project. I managed to obtain some grant money from the "Alberta Buck for Wildlife Trust Fund" and I also acquired all of the necessary permits and permissions to complete the project. Later on in the spring, I contracted a heavy equipment operator and a large track hoe for the job. I also made arrangements with another contractor that would supply the huge Class 4 and 5 rock, for the fish habitat. These rocks were going to be the size of a Volkswagen car!

Because we would be working in the river channel at low flows, the project was scheduled to take place in the late summer, when water flow volume from the mountains has been reduced. At that point in time, I would also have to contact TransAlta Utilities to arrange for a reduction in flow during the in-stream work. I had already discussed the planned project with them and they had agreed to help out with the flows.

By the early fall of 1987, the in-stream work had been completed according to plan. The enhanced boulder site would be monitored over the years to assess the structures integrity and its effectiveness in creating habitat for sport fish under low flow conditions. The most important thing to watch for was how the boulders held up to the ice and spring flows in the river.

Over the years following the project, I returned to the site to take a few photos and make some notes on how the boulder site was holding up. I also fished the site on numerous occasions, with good success. The fish were definitely adapting to the boulders for cover under low flows in the river. The scouring effect created by flow around the boulders had resulted in some good pocket water where trout and mountain whitefish would hold.

However, there were a few things that I thought could be changed if I had the opportunity. The first was that the boulders were located too close to the shoreline and under low flow conditions there was not optimal flow to get the best result. The other concern was that the rocks, although they had been seated into the riverbed, were too high above it when the river levels were down. If there was ever another project planned for the river, I could modify the site to make it more effective.

The opportunity to do just that came about in 1996. It was my last year as fish habitat chairman with the JP Chapter of Trout Unlimited and to leave the position satisfied that I had done all that I could during my term, in 1995 I arranged for another boulder enhancement project for the Bow River. This one would be far larger than the first and hopefully with more funding to carry out the work.

I prepared a proposal for the creation of five major boulder sites starting just upstream of the Highway 22 Bridge in Cochrane and ending approximately three kilometers downstream. In need of a lot more money than the first project, I approached a few corporate sponsors to participate in the program, along with the Alberta Conservation Association. The Jumpingpound Chapter of TU would put up $2,500.00 to get things started. TransAlta Utilities Corporation was providing the majority of funding for the project and Atco Pipelines contributed as well.

The ACA money would be used to modify the 1987 site to make it more effective as fish habitat. With heavy equipment already in the river and having to pass the 1987 site while moving upstream, the cost for modification would be minimal. Sheldon Lowe once again completed a design for the enhancement work. It would be different than the 1987 design and would consist of triple rock placements, 1/3 the distance of the river width, out into the channel. This would insure that adequate flows would pass over the boulders while under low flow conditions.

I managed to find some good sized rocks for the majority of the project around Cochrane, large good quality sandstone. Both the Town of Cochrane, Operational Services and Burnco Ltd. helped move the rocks close in to the different sites. The balance of the Class 4 rock would come in from a quarry in Exshaw, to the west of Cochrane. The costs for bringing in rock had increase substantially since the 1987 project.

As was done in the 1987 project, TransAlta Utilities would hold the water back in the river channel during part of the morning work program. This project would take a few more days than the first one, so it was determined that we would start at the lower site and work upstream in the morning hours, over a three day period. A heavy duty 980 Cat loader would be used to move spoil out of the river channel and also transport the heavy rocks to the track hoe for placement in the river channel.

By the mid summer period of 1996, all of the necessary permits and permissions had been obtained and the contractor with the equipment was secured for the in-stream work window that had been specified by Alberta Environment. The JP Chapter members were anxious to have the program underway; this was a big one for the club. It had been three years before that they had completed the trapping program on the JP Creek and they were ready for another major achievement.

Finally, on August 16th, the project started. The first site was located on the west bank of the river on an island locally known as Griffin's Island, just east of the Town of Cochrane. The loader started early in the morning by moving the rocks that were to be used, from a staging point off the island to the high bank of the river. From there, the track hoe could take the boulder and place it in the riverbed, positioned in a slight depression that the excavator had made to seat in the boulders.

A small pocket pool was excavated directly below some of the boulder clusters as an experiment to see if they maintained their depth in the following years. These pocket pools would provide additional habitat for sport fish under both high and low flows in the river channel.

By mid morning, the first site was competed. While the track hoe walked up the river channel to the next site, the loader did some reclamation work to cover its tracks and lessen any disturbances on the access trail.

Fortunately, I had two very good operators on the equipment. The track hoe operator, Dave Lange, had experience on building retaining walls with large quarry rock and he was a real pro at handling the large boulders with his bucket and hydraulic thumb.

Later on in the project, Dave had to crawl up a very steep bank with the hoe and then go over a small pipeline without touching the ground with his tracks. He completed both obstacles with ease. You really have to see this to understand what I'm talking about. The pipeline crossing is done by using heavy timbers on either side of the buried pipe. By using the bucket and boom of the hoe, an operator can tip up the tracks of the hoe and walk it ahead until he can lower the tracks onto the timber on the far side of the pipeline.

Track hoe operators use this same technique when they travel over sidewalks in new housing developments. Dave traveled up a very steep bank by using the bucket and boom of the machine to pull him and the equipment up the slope. You really have to know your business for this operation, there is a lot of balance involved. The whole thing was very interesting for me to watch.

Above Photo: Operator Dave Lange walks the track hoe over a pipeline crossing, using timbers on both sides of the buried pipe.

After that first day, we had completed two of the five sites on the river. I was relieved that everything had gone so well. This is the most difficult time of any fish habitat enhancement project, the first day. Once you have got things underway, there is always a load off your shoulders. Especially if everything goes according to plan!

By the third day, all of the sites had been completed. However, I had been monitoring the sites under high water flows and some of the boulders were submerged but too close to the surface for my liking. I made a decision at that point in time to haul the track hoe back down to the first site and take care of this situation. It is a difficult call but necessary under the circumstances. I had liability concerns that if the boulders were too close to the surface, they may be a hazard to canoeists or other boaters traveling the river when the water levels were high.

It took half a day to correct the situation and after it was done I was very satisfied with my decision. If I hadn't completed the project to my standards that first go around, I could not have slept at night, worrying about the consequences. After this correction the project was completed, a little over budget ($1,200.00) but finished.

I got Cochrane Trophy and Engraving to make up a very nice bronze sign for the Highway 22 boulder site parking lot. Daryl Vinsent and Andy Macri did a good job of seating the new sign into a very large sandstone boulder that bordered the parking lot.

It has been 10 years since that project was completed on the Bow River in Cochrane. I have fished the boulder sites on many occasions, with good success on most outings. I love the challenge of fishing the sites, with the counter acting currents that make fly fishing a dry fly so difficult.

There is tremendous gratification in knowing that, thanks to a small grass roots group of people and their efforts, some major changes have been made in our beloved and "not so famous" reach of the Bow River. The beautiful JP strain of Bow River trout are now under special protective regulations and the low water habitat in the area that they congregate in, during the spring of the year has now been improved.

In the years following the last project that I completed for the JP Chapter, the club slowly folded. Membership dropped and I think that there was no sense of direction and projects to keep everyone content. In any case, the people involved over the four or five years after the club formed can be proud of their accomplishments in the area and rest assured that their efforts have made a real difference in our area fishery.

Above Photo: This is a photo of a triple rock placement under low flows on the Bow River in Cochrane. The picture was taken 10 years after the projects completion.

Some Closing Thoughts

It is my hope that you will gain some enjoyment and knowledge from this book. With the advent of new regulations for fishing without bait on many waters in this area, I felt that it was important to provide some angling alternatives for those that love to fish streams and lakes as much as I do.

Since I started fly fishing over 40 years ago, I have learned that angling for fish without bait can produce very good results and further to that the use of single barbless hooks is not a major setback for anglers that catch fish. If you keep the right tension on your line and play the fish properly, you can land your catch more often than not.

There is no reason why an angler that fishes with a spinning or spin casting rod and reel cannot effectively fish a streamer or nymph fly pattern. By following the contents of the chapter on fishing a fly or jig, you should be able to effectively fish most waters for trout, whitefish and pike.

Good angling and remember, it is the experience and the environment in which you enjoy your sport that provides the best part of your memories on the water!

Yours truly,
Guy Woods

A photo of the author Guy Woods holding a 17.lb steelhead, caught on the Quinsum River, near Cambell River, BC in 1990.

A note about the author

The author lives in the Town of Cochrane, Alberta, just a few blocks from the banks of the Bow River. He has spent a better part of his life fishing the Bow and other area trout waters over the last 40 years.

He was an outdoor columnist for the "Cochrane This Week" for four years in the 1980's and has written over 30 freelance magazine articles relating to the outdoors.

Guy is Director of Bow Valley Habitat Development, a consulting firm that specializes in stream reclamation and fish habitat enhancement work. BVHD has completed over 30 major fish habitat enhancement projects in the province of Alberta, starting in 1987.

When he has free time, you can expect to find him fly fishing somewhere in these parts or enjoying some other form of outdoor recreation. He also fills in some spare hours as a fly fishing and fly tying instructor, writing or managing a few trout ponds located in the Town of Cochrane.

Presently, BVHD is spearheading a major stream reclamation and fish habitat enhancement program on "Millennium Creek", in the Town of Cochrane. The project was started in 2005 and it is near being completed.

Guy hopes to start work on another book in the near future, that will focus on fly fishing and will most likely include some more stories about the enhancement work that he is involved in.